What people say about Paul McGee's SUMO presentations and workshops...

'I've absolutely no doubt that your approach can help build resilience and enhance the quality of people's lives. The clarity and simplicity of your explanations are accessible to everyone, and I know many patients who would benefit from adopting this approach.
You use SUMO as a way of having a legitimate and life-enhancing conversation with ourselves, forcing us to reflect and aim for what really matters.'
Dr Phil Hammond
GP, journalist, and broadcaster

'You inspired the audience with your SUMO techniques. You were practical, motivational, and entertaining.'
Miles Standish
Managing Director, UK Life and Pensions,
Towry Law Group

'The feedback has been unbelievable! Delegates were using some of the seven questions during the conference. Lots of fun, but at the same time, lots of learning.'
Philip Turner
Operations Director, NHS

D0190466

What people say about Paul McGee's SUMO book...

'The SUMO approach is powerful, simple and effective. Anyone who reads it is sure to look at themselves and the world differently as a result.'
Octavius Black and Sebastian Bailey
Co-founder of The Mind Gym

'Don't be deceived by this book's simple approach. Beneath the surface it's packed with wisdom and insights communicated in a practical, humourous, and inspirational way. Make sure you read it.'
Haydn Roberts
Head of Player Care and Support,
Manchester City Football Club

'We live in a complex world. Paul McGee's messages stand out because they're clear, simple, and above all they work. We have a short time on this planet and we need to make the most of it. SUMO shows you how. By applying these ideas I believe you can make a BIG difference in every area of your life, personally and professionally.'
Marie Mosely
Business Psychologist

'Paul's SUMO principles are essential life tools, nothing less. I refer to his seven questions on an almost daily basis. They have been massively useful for dealing with issues both personally and professionally. Paul, I cannot thank you enough.'

David Thomas
International speaker, author, and
memory world record holder

'SUMO is a brilliant book, packed with simple, inspirational, and innovative ideas that can be applied to any aspect of your life, whether it be personal, business, or recreational. Paul's knowledge, enthusiasm, and ability to clearly explain these methods is unsurpassed. I heartily recommend this excellent read.'

Professor Damian Hughes
Sports Psychology Consultant to Great Britain,
England, and Warrington Wolves Rugby League

'I can honestly say no other book has had such a profound effect on my life. I have had all my family and friends read it, and it has become my mission in life to spread the principles to everyone I meet. If only everyone read SUMO the world would be a better place.'

Kevin Wickson
Service Director, PESL

'The one thing that stands out in the book is how Paul addresses the steps to success with clarity and ease, in the most simple language. I will recommend the book to people I know, because like me they will appreciate the practical wisdom.'

Sudakshin Susarla
Chennai, India

'I started the book on a flight to France and have just finished it on a train from London.
I did more than enjoy it... I loved it.
I have read many of these books, and spent many a motorway mile listening to Steven Covey and others, but was all too often left a little cynical.
I think including the personal stuff was brave but brilliant.
It would be all too easy to preach the gospel and not document the journey.
Finally here was a book written for someone like me by someone like me.'

Stuart Brown
Managing Director, Ten Alps Publishing

SUMO
(Shut Up, Move On)

The straight talking guide to succeeding in life

10th Anniversary Edition

By Paul McGee

Illustrations by Fiona Osborne

CAPSTONE

Library of Congress Cataloging-in-Publication Data

McGee, Paul, 1964-
    S.U.M.O (Shut up, move on) : the straight-talking guide to succeeding in life / Paul McGee.
— 10th anniversary edition.
        pages cm
    Includes index.
        ISBN 978-0-85708-622-8 (paperback)   1. Self-actualization (Psychology)   I. Title.
II. Title: Shut up, move on.
    BF637.S4M3915 2015
    158.1—dc23
                                                                                    2015002041

A catalogue record for this book is available from the British Library.

ISBN 978-0-857-08622-8 (pbk)
ISBN 978-0-857-08620-4 (ebk)   ISBN 978-0-857-08621-1 (ebk)

Cover design: Wiley
Cover illustration: Fiona Osborne

Set in 11/16 Frutiger LT Std by Aptara

Printed in Great Britain by TJ International Ltd, Padstow, Cornwall, UK

Dedication

To Paul 'The Philosopher'
with deep gratitude and appreciation
for sharing your friendship, wisdom and laughter.
From The Sumo Guy

Proverbs 18.24

Contents

About the Author

Photo by Andy Preston

PAUL McGEE is an international speaker, a bestselling author and performance coach. He's Managing Director of his own training and education company and also the proud creator of SUMO (Shut Up, Move On®).

Paul's main aim is to help people achieve better results in life, whilst having more fun in the process. He has shared his SUMO message in 40 countries around the globe to date. Paul works with major organizations in both public and private sectors and as a performance coach with Manchester City Football Club. His academic background is in psychology, and his early career was spent working in Human Resources with Unilever.

Originally from Manchester, he enjoys comedy, football and being around people who make him think. An avid lover of sunshine, his aim is to spend more time working and chilling out in Australia.

He is married to Helen and has two children, Matt and Ruth, who are his biggest teachers in life, keep him grounded and remind him not to take himself too seriously.

Preface to the 10th Anniversary Edition

It was the spring of 2005. I sat at my kitchen table overlooking my garden, making some final changes to the draft of my *SUMO* book. It was the first time I'd worked with my publisher, Capstone, and it was exciting to do so. But no one was fooling themselves. My editor knew he was taking a chance working on such a book. Thirteen publishers had already turned down the opportunity to publish *SUMO*. As one editor put it so directly… 'no one is going to walk into a bookshop and buy a book that's telling them to Shut Up, Move On. A book title has to work from the outset, and Paul, yours just doesn't.'

Despite my passion for what I was writing I had some genuine concerns. Was anyone really going to take seriously a book that encouraged 'Fruity Thinking,' said Hippo Time was OK and that we might want to Ditch Doris Day? I had my doubts, but I chose to allow them to occupy the seats at the back of my mind. The seats at the front were where hope and expectation sat. However, doubt was sometimes encouraged to take centre stage by some well-meaning friends who sensitively asked 'What will you do if it's a flop? How will you cope with the disappointment?' Who needs enemies, eh?

My mentor and best mate Paul Sandham was slightly more encouraging: 'You've got a unique, quirky style bud. It won't be to everyone's taste, but it will connect with more people than you realize. Just make sure you share your struggles, not just your successes. That's what will make this book different.' So I did.

As you'll discover, I've sought to add some colour and context to what you're about to read. My goal is not just simply to share some ideas, but to highlight how these ideas have helped me overcome some of my own challenges. Ten years on from its first publication, it seems my mate Paul had a point – people connect with stories. People not only read mine, but contacted me to share theirs. You see, I realize that although we may never have met, we do have things in common. Most of us are not celebrities. We're not chased by the paparazzi. Our photos don't appear in magazines. Our weight gain or weight loss is not a source of news for the gossip columns. But we all have our own story – something that is significant to us personally. We're all still of equal importance even if that doesn't equate to equal profile. Ultimately, we're all on a similar journey. It's called life.

We have our dreams. We have our disappointments. We're full of hope. We also get hurt. We fall. We get back up. We press on. We give up. We wake up happy. We wake up sad. We delight in the company of friends and family. We despair when we feel rejected and alone. Life, at times, seems utterly amazing and at other times appears to make no sense. Our relationships are our biggest source of pleasure and also our biggest source of pain. We sometimes savour the special moments but sleepwalk through the majority of them. We feel we're capable of anything but our doubts are our constant companions. We surprise ourselves. We despair of ourselves.

So, we may be from different places, different backgrounds and be different ages, but we still have so much in common. It's what we have in common that seems to connect with the readers of this book. Deep down I sensed it would. How could I be so sure?

Well, I don't just write about the SUMO message. I speak about it too. As I write the preface to this 10th anniversary edition, the number of countries I've shared these ideas in has reached 40. Tens of thousands of people have heard this message. A few have ridiculed both me and my ideas. But most have related to them. My message, I feel humbled to say, has resonated with people across all ages, from all backgrounds and amongst all cultures. Not everyone gets my humour. You'll see why later. But many do connect with some, if not all, of what I'm saying.

Yet, if you're reading this book for the first time, you're reading it in a world that is vastly different from the world of those who first opened these pages back in 2005. What we now take for granted as very much part of our everyday lives was either in its infancy or did not even exist when this book was first published. On Facebook? Me too. But its creator Mark Zuckerberg only developed it in 2004. In 2005 it was only available to college students in the United States. When *SUMO* was first published, it's likely only a few people outside of the US had heard of Facebook. Yet today it has so many users that if Facebook was a country it would be the third largest on the planet behind China and India. In 2005 you called people 'friends' because you actually knew them.

What about Twitter? I love to tweet (@thesumoguy if you want to connect). Back in 2005 no one had heard of it, let alone used it. Why? Twitter wasn't launched until July 2006.

What about YouTube? In 2005 the domain name was secured, but no videos were uploaded until later in the year. It wasn't launched in the UK until my wife's birthday, June 19th 2007. To be fair, I don't think my wife's birthday had much to do with the launch, but I so wished I'd filmed her at our romantic meal out near the monkey enclosure at Chester Zoo that day. If I had, you would have been able to witness for yourself the look of joy on her face as we chilled out with the baboons and gorillas while we ate our cheese and pickle sandwiches and consumed several pork pies. (Yes, you've guessed it, I'm from the north of England.)

The 'financial crisis' was something people remembered happening back in the 1980s and early 1990s. Few, if any, economists back in 2005 were predicting the financial global meltdown that was to take place three years later.

In 2005 you probably also used your watch to tell the time, regretted not having your camera to capture a special moment and simply zoned out when conversations became boring. You see, *SUMO* was first published in a world devoid of iPhones. There were no apps. It was difficult to see photos of what meals your friends had been eating earlier that day. How did we survive? I'm not sure.

Now, a world of immense possibility to enhance both connection and conflict exists because of such technological development and ideas. It has also multiplied, perhaps a hundredfold, the amount of distractions we now accept as being a normal part of our day-to-day lives. Why reflect when I can tweet? Why converse with the people I'm with when I can connect with 'friends' I've never met? Why engage with my children when I can place headphones on them and sit them in front of an iPad?

If there's one word to sum up the last decade it would not be change. That's too obvious. No, the word would be 'relentless'. A relentless amount of change, happening at a relentless speed where standing still means you're going backwards and staying in the game means not staying in the same place. No human being that's ever walked upon this planet in previous generations has had to deal with the relentless pace of life and change we now take for granted. Life, for many people, is like being on a rollercoaster which never stops and the brakes are no longer working.

This is our current reality, and as such I think the SUMO message is perhaps even more relevant and applicable to life now than it was when it was first published ten years ago. Here's why I think that's the case. If you and I are to maximize our potential and the opportunities that life has for us, there are several factors which I believe will contribute to this. Each one is, to some extent, explored within the SUMO approach. Let me give you a brief overview of what these factors are.

Reflection. At the heart of SUMO is the call to get off auto-pilot; to stop and press pause. Our relentlessly fast-paced, busy and distraction-filled world does not encourage this. People now pay thousands of pounds to escape the noise of the world – to find silence. SUMO, however, will help you to reflect in a very honest and practical way about a number of aspects of your life. Some of these reflections will bring you reassurance, but others may cause you to reconsider your priorities and current behaviour. The SUMO challenge is to live with increased awareness, attention and appreciation.

As the Latin writer Publilius Syrus said, 'Awareness, not age, leads to wisdom.' Reflection gives you the opportunity to become more self-aware.

Recovery. The pace of change and the tidal wave of distractions can be exhausting. Not just physically, but, perhaps even more importantly, mentally. Modern technology means we are more accessible than ever before. But this, in turn, means we're finding it increasingly difficult to switch off. I don't know what it's like for women, but I'm increasingly seeing guys on their mobile phones whilst relieving themselves at the urinal. I've eavesdropped on some very interesting conversations whilst taking a comfort break at various service stations throughout the UK.

The reality is our minds are being constantly stimulated. We're not allowing ourselves to press pause and take time out. And despite the mental fatigue that this brings, more and more people are reporting difficulty in sleeping.

I work with a Premiership football team. These elite sportspeople need to be in peak physical and mental condition. And what might surprise some people is the important role recovery time plays in this. It's built into their training programme. It's not a nice option – it's a necessity.

You might not be an elite sportsperson, but you're about to discover that the SUMO approach encourages us to build recovery time into our own lives.

Perhaps we need to take a lesson from the airlines. In their safety announcements they always state the following: If there's a drop in cabin pressure, put your oxygen mask on first *before* helping others.

Responsibility. More than any other animal humans are hugely dependent on others for our survival when we're born. But some people believe they can live their whole lives relying on others to meet their needs. People can develop a sense of entitlement that the world owes them a living, that teachers, employers and governments should take responsibility for our welfare and well-being.

Well, here's the deal. This way of thinking will seriously undermine a person's ability to make the most of their time on this planet. As you'll discover, taking personal responsibility (whilst still being open to support from others) will be the cornerstone to you achieving the life you want.

Resilience. We mentioned earlier that life at times can be described as a rollercoaster. It has both ups and downs. However, it's how you deal with the down times, the setbacks, the challenges and disappointments that influences whether such events derail you or drive you on to succeed. Throughout this book, and particularly in one chapter, you'll discover how to develop resilience when the going gets tough.

Relationships. The quality of your life is determined by the quality of your relationships. That's true in both your personal and professional life. The people in your world play a significant role in influencing how you see yourself and the opportunities life can offer. As I mentioned earlier, these relationships will be your biggest source of joy. They'll also be your biggest source of pain. Either way, relationships are the bedrock of our lives and there are ways to enhance them.

Let me be very clear on this. Good relationships are not simply a matter of luck. As you'll discover, the SUMO approach will explore a simple visual metaphor that thousands of people claim has helped them reduce conflict, communicate more clearly and build better relationships with others. Of course, simply reading about it won't magically and mysteriously cause relationships to succeed. But taking action and applying the insights will increase your chances.

Resourcefulness. Lots of things are nice to have. I would like to go into McDonalds and order a lobster thermidor. But it's not on the menu.

Sadly, some people spend time and energy focusing on what is not on their menu – in other words, they focus on what isn't in their lives rather than what is. Now, not only is this deeply dissatisfying and demotivating, it distracts you from the positive things that are happening in your life and the many skills and abilities you have. The SUMO approach helps us understand the importance of where we choose to focus our attention. The challenge is not to see ourselves as a helpless victim, but as someone who, with the help of others, can discover inner resources and develop new ones to meet the challenges of life.

As you'll discover, the key is to explore and focus on the range of possibilities and options for moving forward rather than being sucked into simply obsessing over problems.

Reality. I'm sometimes referred to as a motivational speaker. That's a term which sends some people reaching for the sick bucket. Perhaps these people view motivational speakers as out of touch with reality, having an approach to life which is superficial at best and dangerous at worst. It's more 'rah-rah' than reality. Well, firstly I acknowledge there are some speakers like that. But many aren't – they offer both inspiration and ideas to encourage and equip people.

I do all I can to ensure I fall into this latter category. In fact, I trademarked the term 'Mancunian Motivation' (Mancunian is a term used to describe people from Manchester). Mancunian motivation is simply summed up by the following approach:

Tell it as it is. No bull. Let's be really practical.

This is what I endeavour to do in this book. The success of the SUMO approach stems from the fact that it's grounded in reality. You're encouraged to deal with life as it is, rather than as you'd like it to be.

So these seven factors – reflection, recovery, responsibility, resilience, relationships, resourcefulness and reality – are all crucial to us achieving better results in life. What you read will not be the panacea to all your problems. Neither is this the only book you'll need to read to develop the skills and character required to meet the challenges of life as it is now. But I genuinely believe the SUMO approach can help. It will contribute ideas and provide some inspiration to support you on the journey. Perhaps the fact that this is the 10th anniversary edition is testament to that.

Over these last ten years I've heard from people from around the world who have come across my book and been helped by it. It's humbling to read their stories, particularly when I might be facing some challenges of my own at the time. In the UK alone, sales have surpassed 60,000, and I know many more people have read *SUMO* after it was passed on to them by a friend. I do celebrate its success and recognize the support I've received from others, but I also hope it goes on to help many more people who will find value in these simple but powerful approaches to dealing with life. Perhaps after you've read it you'll pass on a copy to someone else, or simply share some of the insights you've gained.

So much has changed in the last ten years, and whatever the next decade holds for you and me, I hope what you're about to read makes a real and long-lasting difference.

Enjoy the journey. And make a difference.

Paul McGee
2015

Introduction

'You don't have to be ill to get better.'

Eric Berne

I spent 13 years at school. I learnt a lot. I learnt about algebra, how to use a Bunsen burner, how bad I am at woodwork, a few things about dinosaurs and the joys of life under the Romans. On reflection, though, I don't feel I learnt much about life and how to make the most of it. I explored the inner workings of a frog, but I never learnt about how to understand myself and other people. I learnt to stand up when a teacher came into the room and to hand in my homework on time if I wanted to avoid detention. But I wasn't taught how to set goals, manage my emotions or how to handle conflict. For me, school prepared me for exams. It didn't prepare me for life. I appreciate a lot has probably changed in education now, but that was my experience.

If you asked me a few years ago, 'would you like your life to be a brilliant and wonderful experience both for you and those around you?' I would have answered a resounding 'yes'. However, if you then asked me how I intended to make this happen, I would probably have waffled on for several minutes before coming to the conclusion 'I'm not so sure'. But I've learnt a lot over the last few years. My answer now would be very different.

Over these next seven chapters, you will get to hear what my answers are. They are based on over twenty-five years studying psychology, running my own business and, more importantly, my observations and conversations with tens of thousands of people. My job as a professional speaker and my experience of running seminars on subjects related to 'change, motivation and relationships' have given me a fascinating insight into what does and doesn't work in people's lives. My work has taken me from Tanzania to Todmorden, from Hong Kong to Halifax, from India to Islington and from Malaysia to Manchester. Whatever the country, whatever the culture, I learnt this – people are basically the same. They have similar hopes, dreams and challenges. They want to improve their lives, be happy and create a better future for their children. Of course there are differences, but if you dig beneath the surface, you find overwhelming similarities.

Why SUMO?

A few years ago I came across the phrase SUMO. I don't recall who said it but I do remember what it stood for – **S**hut **U**p, **M**ove **O**n. To some people this seems like a rather aggressive statement, but let me explain what I mean when I say 'Shut Up, Move On'. Firstly, I am not suggesting people simply need to 'get over it' or 'pull themselves together' (although there may be occasions when both of these responses are necessary). Neither does it mean 'forgive and forget' or 'just ignore reality and get on with life'.

SUMO, for me, captures the essence of what I believe are the key truths around success and fulfilment. Let me elaborate.

When I was a child I learnt the Green Cross Code. It was a code intended to keep children safe when crossing the road. I learnt the phrase 'Stop, Look and Listen'. When I use the words 'Shut Up', I am encouraging people to *stop* what they're doing, take some time out and *look* at their lives and reflect on how they are thinking and behaving. I want people to *listen*. Yes, be prepared to listen to others but, more importantly, listen to yourself. Go beyond the noise-filled, activity-driven, fast-paced existence of daily life and spend some time alone with your own thoughts.

'Shut Up' also means 'let go'. As you read this book, there may be views and opinions you have about life that you have clung onto simply through habit. My goal is to challenge you to consider whether your outlook on life is helping or hindering you.

In recent years we've sometimes substituted the phrase 'Stop, Understand' for 'Shut Up'. A less provocative phrase, it still captures the essence of SUMO. It pays to take time out to Stop and Understand who we are, where we're heading and what we need, or don't need, to get us there.

The 'Move On' part of SUMO is saying a number of things. It is meant as encouragement that whatever your past experiences, your future doesn't have to be the same. Tomorrow can be different from today – if you want it to be. Move On is asking you to look at your future, to see the possibilities that lie ahead rather than be stuck in the reality of your current circumstances. It's a call to take action, to do something. It's a challenge not to 'think on' but 'Move On' and we'll look at ways to make that happen.

The phrase SUMO now underpins my personal philosophy on how to make the most of life. It is a challenging phrase, but it's also one that is meant to encourage and inspire you both in your work and personal life. Hopefully, it's a phrase you will always remember. In Latin SUMO means 'choose' and I sincerely hope what you're about to read will help you make some wise choices in every aspect of your life.

Let me explain my approach in writing this book. Firstly, I have aimed to make the concepts I write about memorable. For instance, I'm convinced there is not a book in the world that has the concept 'Ditch Doris Day'. I have also included sections called 'The personal stuff'. It's not compulsory that you read these sections, but I believe they bring life – and colour and context – to what we're exploring. They also reveal my own struggles and occasional successes as I wrestle with applying these ideas to my own life.

To help you engage further with the material, I ask a number of questions. Your experience of this book will be richer and more revealing and rewarding when you spend some time, however briefly, chewing over your answers.

I've also sought to make the material simple and accessible (so much so that my organization now works in both primary and secondary schools helping children use the principles). But behind the simplicity are some well-tested and tried tools and

5

methodologies: Cognitive Behavioural Therapy, Solution Focused Therapy, Appreciative Inquiry and the work of the positive psychology movement all underpin my work. But relax. You don't need an understanding of any of these in order to benefit from this book. So, whatever your background or your experience of reading this kind of book, my goal is simple – I want to provide ideas and insights that you can use. Immediately.

Finally, although you might not notice, I have tried to add some humour. The ideas we look at are very important, but that doesn't mean we cannot have the occasional smile. I hope you agree.

Enjoy.

Chapter 1

E + R = O

H as anyone ever said something to you and you've thought, 'Well that's just common sense'? Or have you ever made a discovery about how things work and thought 'Why didn't I think of that before'?

Me too. In fact I guess we all have. One such incident happened to me whilst I was in my late twenties. I was listening to the author and speaker Jack Canfield explain a concept that had a profound impact on how I saw the world and dealt with situations. On reflection I realize that most people will think that what Canfield said was 'just common sense' and 'fairly obvious'. And maybe they're right. But here's the interesting part. Until that moment it hadn't been common sense to me and it wasn't obvious until it was pointed out.

So what was this insight, this idea that has had such a profound impact? I guess you could call it a formula for life. For me it's become the foundation upon which my SUMO principles are based.

The formula is simply this: $E + R = O$.

Now, in order to explain the formula and why understanding it is crucial to our lives, let's explore a scenario.

Imagine you're driving in the fast lane of the motorway, when you notice a car flashing its headlights at you. It's clear from their aggressive driving that they are not pointing out your car needs washing or you forgot your change at the toll booth. No. The driver behind you is in a hurry and you're in their way.

So what do you do?

I asked that question to a group of twelve managers I was working with. As you read their responses ask yourself which, if any, you can relate to.

Karl said he would refuse to be intimidated, maintain his current speed and not pull over for the driver behind him. He may even use a particular hand signal to highlight the fact that he didn't appreciate the other driver's behaviour.

There were nods of approval from other members of the group.

Brian interjected.

'Guys I can't believe what you're suggesting; I'd simply move in at an appropriate time and allow them to overtake me...'

Before he could finish his sentence pandemonium broke out around the room.

'No way would you do that Brian. I've been in a car with you,' said his colleague Darran. 'I know how you drive. It's like a battle out there when the traffic's busy and there's just no way you would react in such a calm and submissive manner.'

'And quite frankly I wouldn't want you to,' piped up another colleague.

Brian, clearly enjoying the reaction of his colleagues to what he'd said, added, 'Hey, let me finish. That's not the whole story. After the car had overtaken me I'd immediately pull back out into that lane and flash my lights at them!'

The room erupted into laughter.

The energy and emotion in the group was quite extraordinary. A simple scenario had provoked such an animated reaction.

Then Linda spoke up.

'Guys I've never seen such high levels of testosterone bouncing around the room. You remind me of a group of monkeys on heat.'

There was more laughter.

'Seriously though guys,' Linda continued, 'what Paul's just given us as a scenario happens a lot in our job. But whilst you lot are getting het up and animated about such an event, I'm using the same situation as my chuckle time.'

Linda's colleagues (all of whom were male) calmed down momentarily and looked intrigued and perhaps slightly bemused by Linda's introduction to the discussion of the phrase 'chuckle time'.

'You see, whilst you bunch of primates are seeing your blood pressure rise and your aggression levels soar, I'm having a laugh.'

'OK Linda,' I interrupted. 'You need to put us out of our misery. What exactly is chuckle time?'

'It's quite simply this. In my experience most people who drive aggressively, flashing their lights and tailgating you, are men. And they're usually men in big cars. Now I've got a theory about men who drive big cars. So when they start flashing their lights and start driving in an intimidating way I will signal and move over. However, when they drive past me I will take a momentary glance in their direction and think "small penis". You know what? It makes me chuckle every time.'

There were a few smiles in the room when Linda finished but no audible laughs. Linda's way of dealing with a situation that was common to all of them seemed to put her colleagues' reaction into perspective. I broke the silence and the slight tension building in the room.

'Well thanks for sharing that Linda. I'm just relieved I drive a mini.'

The room erupted into laughter again.

With her humorous insight Linda had made a valuable point, and one that brilliantly illustrates E + R = O. Quite simply it's this: it's not the Event but also how I Respond that influences the Outcome.

It's not an aggressive driver that's influencing my outcome but how I'm responding. One response can lead to stress and confrontation, whilst another can lead to a calmer journey.

Common sense? Obvious? Perhaps. But in my experience very few people live their lives with an awareness of such a formula. For many years I certainly didn't.

11

In fact many people seem to live their lives by an alternative one: E = O. In other words, the outcomes in my life are down entirely to whatever events I've experienced. I have no control. Certain events will trigger certain outcomes. Period.

SUMO wisdom

Life is rarely just about what happens to you. It's how you respond that makes the difference.

What Events have you experienced?

Have you ever faced any of the following in your life? (Simply tick 'yes' or 'no')

	Yes	No
Been made redundant	☐	☐
Experienced significant change at work	☐	☐
Not achieved your expected grades at school	☐	☐
Over-reacted to a situation and then regretted what you said and did	☐	☐
Failed your driving test	☐	☐
Been dumped by someone you loved	☐	☐
Applied for a job and not got an interview	☐	☐
Missed out on the house of your dreams through no fault of your own	☐	☐
Found someone driving aggressively behind you	☐	☐
Felt badly let down by a family member or close friend	☐	☐

It would be surprising if, of the above scenarios, you hadn't experienced at least a few of them.

You see, life is full of events. It's full of opportunities, challenges, setbacks and even some dull, boring moments at times.

But it's not the events alone that determine your outcomes.

It's how you respond.

Succeeding in life is therefore not a matter of chance; it's not whether fate, luck or destiny bestows upon you a set of favourable events. It's about the choices *you* make.

What influences your response?

OK, let's get off auto-pilot for a moment, press pause and explore why we respond the way we do to events and how those responses impact our outcomes. Let's focus on three reasons in particular.

1 Habits... are they helping or hindering you?

As you will discover in the SUMO principle 'Remember the Beachball', a whole host of factors influence how we see the world and therefore how we respond to what we see. Interestingly, the filters through which we see the world have been shaped, influenced and coloured by a number of factors that many of us are now oblivious to.

Our responses to situations have now become habits; habits which were not necessarily consciously chosen but acquired unconsciously over time.

That's why, even when we begin to understand the impact our responses have on our outcomes, it's still not easy to change them. To put it bluntly, our habits can handicap us and prevent us from succeeding in life.

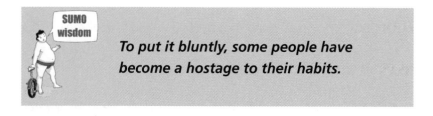

SUMO wisdom

To put it bluntly, some people have become a hostage to their habits.

Let's explore that statement a little further.

Imagine you're off for a walk in the countryside. You come across a field of tall grass; so tall, in fact, that it's higher than you are. You're tired and know that taking a short cut through this field will get you to your destination sooner.

Slowly and tentatively you begin to move forward through the grass and as you do so you begin to leave a pathway behind you. Eventually you make your way across the field and reach your destination.

Now imagine that the next day you go for the same walk and come across the same field of tall grass. You decide to take a short cut across the field. You notice the pathway that you created yesterday. You know it got you to the other side of the field. It might still not be the most direct way through the field – that would be hard to tell without an aerial perspective – but you do know this path will lead to where you want to go.

But you still have a choice. Take the same path as yesterday, or, if you're feeling particularly adventurous, you could create another one.

So what would you do?

What do you think the majority of people do? Create a new path or take the familiar and already established one?

From my experience of human behaviour, most people stick with the path they took the day before. Why? Well, for a start it's easier and the majority of people like solutions that are easy. You also know this path will get you to where you want to be. It's also safer. By taking this route you know what to expect. Now, of course it might not be the quickest route across the field (there could be many others that you've not discovered) but it's a familiar one and the one you're most likely to take.

The brain works in a similar way. When you do a task for the first time the brain begins to establish a series of neural pathways. The more a particular task (or response to an event) occurs, the stronger and more established the neural pathway becomes. That's why deciding to do something differently can sound easy in theory but prove difficult in practice. It's like taking a new path across the field, and unless you see an immediate benefit you're more likely to return to the route (or behaviour) you've previously taken.

Let me give you an example of this. If you were to clasp both hands together you'd notice that one thumb is on top of the other. Try it now. Go on – no one else is watching. In my case it's my right thumb that's on top of my left one.

Now repeat the exercise (and if you're reading this book whilst on a train or plane, do this as subtly as you can without drawing attention to yourself or elbowing the person next to you). However, when you do so, whichever thumb was on the bottom last time (which in my case was my left) put that one on top this time.

Now how does that feel? Strange? For most people it does. And that's how responding differently to events can feel sometimes. It can feel strange; almost not normal. The temptation is to revert back to how we've always responded. We stick with what we feel comfortable with. We go back to our familiar path.

That's absolutely fine when there are no ramifications to your behaviour. Whether your left or right thumb is on top is not going to be the deciding factor in you getting the new job, managing your stress or building a better relationship. But in many cases how you respond to events *will* have ramifications. Just as Linda demonstrated with her story about how she deals with aggressive drivers, people can have very similar events and experiences but have very different outcomes from each other.

Go back to that checklist you completed on page 12. Other people reading this book would have put ticks in the same boxes as you. But just because they've experienced the same event doesn't mean they've had the same outcome. Does it?

Here's the good news. You don't have to become a hostage to your habits. You can create some new pathways. There could be a quicker and better route across the field.

> ## SUMO wisdom
>
> *Just because a path is well worn doesn't make it the best route to take.*

Procrastination is a habit, as is being continually late or losing your temper. But whatever your current habits that are hindering you, you can change. If you genuinely want to respond more effectively to events that happen then look for ideas in this book to create some healthier habits.

Here's the deal. Where you currently find yourself in life has been influenced by your habitual responses to events. And when you change the habits that hinder you and replace them with more helpful ones you will see a change in your outcomes. Things can be different. Just remember it takes time and persistence to create a new pathway and form a new habit. The question is – are you up for the challenge?

Now onto something else worth considering about why we respond the way we do to events.

2 Conditioning (or You, Me and Pavlov's Dog)

Have you ever heard of Pavlov's dog experiment?

Don't worry if you haven't, but that's a question I ask my audiences when I'm speaking.

And I get some strange answers.

They can border on the bizarre. They tend to have a common theme, however – the ringing of a bell is usually mentioned somewhere. However, one person thought the experiment involved dissecting a dog's head, after which when the bell rang the dog's eyes still moved. (I always love working in Yorkshire.) Another believed the experiment involved placing electrodes on a dog's testicles and when the bell rang the dog was either electrocuted or given some food. As the dog didn't know if it would be fed or electrocuted it developed psychosis. Well, to the best of my knowledge neither of the above experiments ever took place – certainly not by Ivan Pavlov anyway.

Here's what did happen.

Pavlov (1849–1936) was a Russian scientist based in St. Petersburg. He studied animal behaviour and one experiment involved him measuring the salivation levels of dogs. He noticed that his dogs' salivation levels increased when they saw food. Just as humans may lick their lips in anticipation of a veritable feast, dogs will salivate. Pavlov took the experiment further. Using a variety of sounds, one of which is commonly believed to be the ringing of a bell, Ivan Pavlov would ring the bell as the dogs were fed. He repeated this over several days – ring the bell, feed the dogs; ring the bell, feed the dogs; ring the bell, feed the dogs. Then came the interesting part. Pavlov then began to ring the bell and not feed the dogs. The bell rang but no food came. The dogs still salivated. He continued the experiment. He kept ringing those bells; there was still no food and the dogs' saliva continued to flow.

The experiment has been referred to as an example of conditioned response. Pavlov's dogs had become conditioned to salivate at the sound of a bell even when there was no food. In other words, their previous experiences had influenced their current responses.

OK, so what has Pavlov's dog experiment (conducted in the 1890s) got to do with you and me living in the 21st century?

Well, quite a lot actually.

You see, in many ways we're a bit like Pavlov's dog. It might not be bells that cause us to salivate, but the media, our education, our upbringing and who we spend time with can all influence or condition how we see and therefore how we respond to our world and the events around us. Some of our responses to events come as automatically as Pavlov's dog salivating at the sound of a bell. Rarely do we think about our response and the reasons why we behave the way we do – we simply tend to operate on auto-pilot – without thinking.

> **SUMO wisdom**
>
> *Some people are sleepwalking through life oblivious to their behaviour or the impact of their responses.*

That's why the whole SUMO approach is designed to help you stop, press pause and think about what outcomes you want in life and how taking control of your responses can create better outcomes for yourself and others.

You see, we need to challenge the lie that says 'I can never change' and learn to recognize we're not simply an upgraded version of Pavlov's dog. Yes, how we've been conditioned to see and understand ourselves and our world can have a profound impact on us, but it doesn't have to be permanent. If we genuinely feel dissatisfied with our current outcomes to events in life then, in a sense, we need to change our conditioner. We can choose to change our mental diet and feed our minds on different information that can positively influence how we see ourselves and the world.

By becoming more aware of why we respond to events the way we do, we can, over time, work on making better responses. This won't happen overnight; the SUMO approach is not a quick-fix instant cure, but it will equip you with ideas and insights to help you break free from what may have been unhelpful and perhaps rigid ways of responding to events.

So that's a brief look at how our conditioning can affect us. Now let's explore a third factor.

3 Emotions... why sensible people do stupid things

I was watching a TV documentary called *Neighbours from Hell*. One episode featured two families, one of which enjoyed bird watching whilst the other family had their elderly mother living with them.

One day the bird-watching family noticed a bird in their garden they had rarely seen before. The father grabbed his binoculars to study the bird. After a while the bird flew into next door's garden.

The father followed the bird through his binoculars. At that precise moment the elderly mother was enjoying a cup of tea in the conservatory. She noticed her neighbour looking into her garden. She spotted the binoculars. She thought she was being spied upon.

Now just stop for a moment and imagine it was you in the conservatory. How would you respond to the fact that it looks like your neighbours are taking a rather unhealthy interest in what you're up to? Would you...

- Ignore it and carry on drinking your tea?
- Leave the conservatory and go into another room?
- Wave at your neighbour?
- Strip off and reveal a part of your body?
- Plant fast-growing conifer trees between your properties in order to protect your privacy?

So what would you do?

And the response of one of the families?

They grew those conifers. In fact, they planted so many that eventually the people who liked bird watching felt like they were living in darkness. The trees grew so tall that they blocked out their sunlight.

So what happened next? Well, they asked their neighbours to trim back the conifers. They refused. The dispute escalated and they ended up fighting a legal battle that went to court. The legal costs for both families totalled over £50,000. It sounds ridiculous doesn't it? But it's true. Perhaps the most revealing insight from the whole episode came when one of the neighbours was interviewed:

'When my mother saw she was being spied upon she was devastated. We had no choice but to grow those conifer trees to protect our privacy.'

Ridiculous? Possibly. Laughable? Maybe. But it happened.

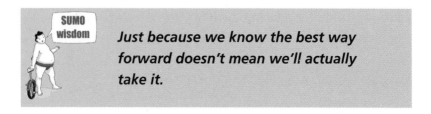

SUMO
wisdom

Just because we know the best way forward doesn't mean we'll actually take it.

Now a different response would have led to a different outcome wouldn't it? Of course it would. But it's revealing that the neighbour felt they 'had no choice'. And here's the key point. Whether we're going through a relationship break-up, have failed an exam, missed out on a promotion or whatever our current challenge or opportunity may be, *we do have a choice* about how we respond. After all, you're not Pavlov's dog.

Now nothing as ridiculous as the above scenario could ever happen in our lives, right? Our minor issues would never escalate into major ones, would they? Well, to be honest it's at this point I start to shuffle uncomfortably in my seat. Fortunately, I get on well with my own neighbours and fast-growing conifers are not an issue. But I have to admit that there are times when, on reflection, I'm left wondering 'Why on earth did I do that?' 'What in the world was I thinking?' 'How could I have been so stupid?'

Can you relate to that?

Or what about the following? Cast your mind back to a time when a friend, family member or colleague told you about an issue they were struggling with. As you listened to them, did you ever find yourself thinking, 'Well the common sense thing to do would be to...' Or thought, 'Well it seems obvious what you've got to do now.' Perhaps you've even offered an opinion that began with the words 'Well if I was you I would...' But have you then found that despite your crystal clear, incisive perspective on what to do they then completely ignore you and do something entirely different?

If so, why is that?

Why is it that something that is common sense and obvious to you seems complex and unclear to someone else? Why is it that you can see that responding differently to an event could create a very different outcome, yet other people live life with their blinkers super glued firmly in place, oblivious to other options and reciting their favourite mantra, 'Well, I had no choice'? Why on earth do so-called intelligent (well, in most cases anyway), rational, experienced people do stupid, irrational things? Why, despite all the opportunities we have, do many people fail to succeed in life?

Ready for the answer? I guess it's obvious when you think about it.

When the event or the problem is happening to someone else, it's easier for you to take a more objective perspective. The less emotionally involved you are, the easier it is to engage your rational brain (we'll look at this in more detail when we explore the SUMO principle 'Develop Fruity Thinking').

But when you're emotionally involved, when the issue affects you or can have a significant impact on someone close to you, then you see things less clearly. You've heard the phrase 'You can't see the wood for the trees', well, another alternative would be 'Your emotions cloud the view to your solution'. It's like trying to complete a jigsaw puzzle through steamed-up glasses – it's possible, but it's not easy.

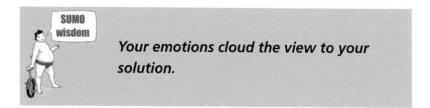

SUMO wisdom

Your emotions cloud the view to your solution.

A way to represent the above would be as follows:

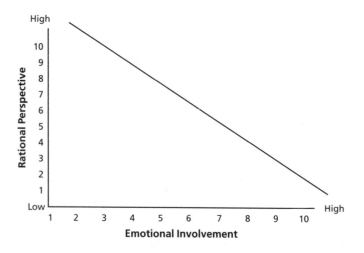

So, when our emotional involvement is low, our rational perspective is high. Conversely, when the emotional involvement is high, our rational perspective is low.

In a nutshell, the equation E + R = O does seem like simplified common sense – and it is. But this insight can, at times, completely bypass our rational minds. It's like saying to a small child as you switch off their bedroom light, 'There's no need to be afraid of the dark.' Rationally you know that to be the case – but you're not the five-year-old who's just watched the latest episode of *Doctor Who* and is left fearing an alien invasion. Emotional engagement in an issue can have the same effect. We become less rational, lose a sense of perspective and our judgement can suffer as a result.

Take some time out now to consider an issue or challenge that you're facing or have recently faced. Think about the equation E + R = O. Now answer the following:

Points to Ponder...

1 *Describe briefly the event.*

2 *Who else was involved?*

3 *How did the event affect you personally?*

4 *On a scale of 1–10 (where 1 = low and 10 = high) how emotionally involved were you?*

25

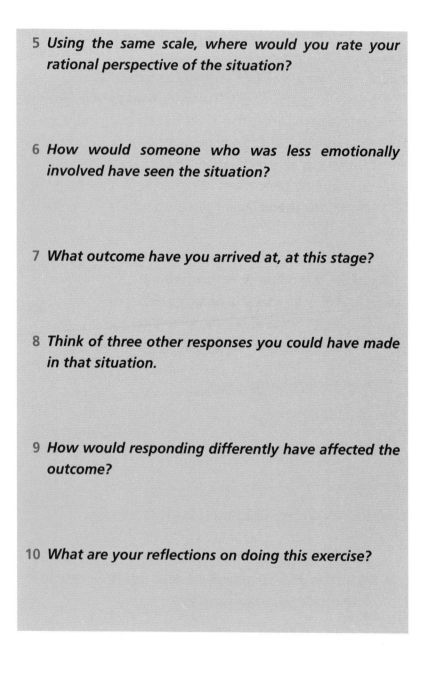

5 *Using the same scale, where would you rate your rational perspective of the situation?*

6 *How would someone who was less emotionally involved have seen the situation?*

7 *What outcome have you arrived at, at this stage?*

8 *Think of three other responses you could have made in that situation.*

9 *How would responding differently have affected the outcome?*

10 *What are your reflections on doing this exercise?*

At the time of writing my daughter Ruth is nineteen. I'm hugely proud of her. Actually I adore her. But pride and adoration don't necessarily always equate to a calm and harmonious relationship. Quite the opposite in fact.

I struggle with clutter. I despise it with a passion. I allow it to stress me. Ruth copes with clutter. So does my wife Helen. Although I may not be the world's tidiest person, I do like things to be tidy. When Ruth chills out in the lounge watching TV, she likes nothing more than a hot chocolate and the occasional piece of fruit. When it's time for bed she leaves the room. Alas, her empty cup and apple core rarely do. That frustrates me. I sometimes make a big issue out of it and demand she comes back down and tidies up after herself. In my emotional state I interpret her behaviour as a lack of respect.

I'm concluding that Ruth believes she can create whatever mess she likes and someone else will clear up after her.

My wife sees it differently. Helen gives a different meaning to the event. The issue of respect or, in this case, a lack of it does not come onto her radar. Forgetfulness and perhaps a slight degree of laziness on Ruth's part are the reasons she believes for the empty cup and apple core. Helen can chill; I can fume. It's the same event but we can experience very different outcomes (as, indeed, can Ruth!). I place a higher importance on the event than Helen does. Therefore I respond differently. But it's just an empty cup and apple core. It's not quite conifer trees and I won't take Ruth to court over the matter (certainly not at this stage anyway) but the seeds have been sown whereby a small and relatively insignificant event has the potential to escalate.

Now if you're a parent reading this, I think you will fall into one of two camps. Some of you do think I've got a point don't you? Ruth should be tidying up after herself. She needs to be taught good habits. Others of you are on the same chill-pill prescription as Helen. You're thinking 'What's the big deal?' Do you know what? Both views are right (you will learn more about this in the SUMO principle 'Remember the Beachball'). The above example is not seeking to determine who is right or wrong but to illustrate how 'events' or other people's behaviour can be perceived or interpreted differently. I guess that's why playwright William Shakespeare wrote in his play *Hamlet*, 'Nothing is either good nor bad, but thinking makes it so.'

So what's the way forward?

We've seen how habits, conditioning and emotions can influence how we 'see' and therefore respond to events, but what do we do now? Are we simply a prisoner to our past – do we really have much control over our future?

Self-awareness can unlock the door to a brilliant life

The key to success is having the awareness to appreciate that, in the words of the French novelist Anaïs Nin, *'we see the world not as it is but as we are'*. It's recognizing that we see events through our own mental filters and give our own meaning to those events – a meaning which may be very different to someone else's. However, the SUMO principles will help you see the events in your life perhaps differently from how you're currently seeing them. They will help you challenge your perception of yourself, other people and life's events.

By seeing differently you can respond differently.

> **SUMO wisdom**
>
> *It's not the event, but the meaning you give the event that determines your response.*

Success is about recognizing the role we play in influencing the outcomes we and others may experience by understanding the effect of *our* responses. Success is about waking up to the fact that the equation to life is not E = O. The Event does not solely determine the Outcome. Our success comes when we become more flexible in our responses and explore alternatives to our usual way of responding.

The journey to success gathers real momentum when we embrace the fact that, in most cases, we can choose both how we will see the event and how we respond. The purpose of the following six SUMO principles is to help you see and understand yourself with greater clarity. The SUMO principles will equip you with insights, ideas and the inspiration to take different actions and make different choices to create better outcomes. They can help lead you to developing healthier habits, to freeing yourself from negative conditioning and to managing your emotions more effectively. If you want to know where the journey to creating and enjoying a brilliant life begins, it begins with the formula E + R = O.

So let's explore our first SUMO principle which will both challenge and equip you to achieve those better outcomes. It's time to Change Your T-shirt. Which Rs does it address?

- *Shut Up* automatic responses, *Move On* to recognizing you can make some different choices.
- *Shut Up* E = O, *Move On* to E + R = O.
- *Shut Up* old harmful habits, *Move On* to making some better new ones.
- *Shut Up* unhelpful conditioning, *Move On* to a new way of seeing the future.
- *Shut Up* being a slave to your emotions, *Move On* to managing them.

SUMO SUMMARY

Chapter 2
Change Your T-shirt

S o let's build upon what we've already been exploring in the previous chapter E + R = O.

Let me start by asking you the same two questions I ask people when I am running a seminar or speaking at a conference. Firstly, 'Do you drive a car?' And secondly, 'Did you get yourself dressed this morning?' If you answered yes to either question you'll relate to the following fact – *much of what we do in life we do without consciously thinking about it.*

Ever had the experience of taking a familiar car journey and suddenly finding yourself at your destination and wondering 'How did I get here?' Or found yourself driving on the motorway and asking yourself, 'What happened to those last ten miles?'

When you got dressed this morning, did you consciously decide in what order to get dressed? Did you weigh up the pros and cons of which shoe to put on first? If not, then you probably identify with the concept I call *'auto-pilot syndrome'*.

We are about to go on a journey. Except on this journey I want you to be very conscious of where you are going and how you get there. To do so, your first step in the SUMO process is to ensure that you take time out, off auto-pilot, and honestly assess how you have been living your life so far. To help you do this, here are three questions to consider.

1 Which person has the biggest influence on your life?
2 Who deserves the most credit for where you currently find yourself in life?
3 Whose advice and opinions do you tend always to act upon?

Let me share with you my answers. (Although I have to confess they would not always have been my responses.)

1 Which person has the biggest influence on your life? *I do.*
2 Who deserves the most credit for where you currently find yourself in life? *I do.*
3 Whose advice and opinions do you tend always to act upon? *My own.*

How do they match yours? I admit there are many people who have influenced my life and who deserve credit for how they have helped me. And I have listened to the advice and opinions of others; but ultimately, the biggest single factor that determines where you and I currently find ourselves in life is 'you'.

SUMO wisdom

If you want to know who is most responsible for where you are in life, take a look in the mirror.

Here is the challenge. We live in a climate and culture where this outlook is not always encouraged.

Be honest. How comfortable do you feel about standing up and saying, 'I take full responsibility for my life?' Well, let's explore why many people would not only feel uncomfortable saying that statement, they would also vehemently disagree with it. I call it the BSE crisis.

The great BSE crisis

I meet individuals who believe that their current circumstances in life have:

1 Nothing to do with the previous decisions they have made.
2 Nothing to do with the actions they have taken.
3 Nothing to do with the attitudes they have adopted.

Apart from that, they take full responsibility for everything.

If life is not as they would want it, they can quickly play their *BSE* card – *B*lame *S*omeone *E*lse. 'I mean, what can I do?' they ask, 'It's not my fault. Someone else is to blame.'

Not only do they carry their own personal BSE card, they also tend to wear a particular T-shirt.

Confused? Let me explain.

Imagine for a moment that how you felt or what you believed about yourself was written on your T-shirt. Some T-shirts may have the phrase 'I am confident' or 'I feel good about myself'; whilst others may have 'I lack self-belief' or 'I don't like people' (I have met a few of those). BSE card carriers, though, wear one with the message – 'Victim'. Wearers of this T-shirt tend to think, say and believe the following:

'This is my life and I must grin and bear it.'

'It's not my fault.'

'Life is not fair.'

'I've never been lucky.'

'I blame the government/my parents/ the traffic/my boss/my teachers/ my kids.'

'I cannot really change or influence my situation.'

'I'm not capable.'

'I'm not confident.'

'I'm not good enough.'

When a group of victim T-shirt wearers get together they hold a 'blame storming' session.

THE PERSONAL STUFF

Have I ever worn the T-shirt? You bet. I failed my Geography A Level and blamed the teachers, until someone pointed out that not every pupil in the class had failed.

In my early days of business I blamed the economy for my lack of success. Things were not buoyant when I began, but it was easier to use the excuse of outside factors than to take a look at my own actions and decisions.

More recently I failed to secure a place as a main speaker at a large sales conference. I had put a great deal of time and effort into persuading the organizers that I was the ideal speaker for this high-profile event. When the 'no thanks' news came through I was gutted, particularly when I found out who had been chosen instead of me. I muttered to myself 'That's not fair... I'm a far better speaker than him.' It took several hours before I realized that I was wearing the Victim T-shirt.

If you had to write a message or slogan that summed up how you currently feel about life, what would it be? Write the word or phrase in the box below.

The message on my T-shirt would be:

It's an interesting exercise isn't it? I've met some people who, judging by their demeanour and outlook, should have a T-shirt that reads 'Miserable Bugger'.

I met one guy, though, and I didn't have to imagine what was on his T-shirt. His view of life was summed up in the following phrase, emblazoned across his T-shirt: 'Same Shit, Different Day'.

I have to confess I asked to see a different doctor next time I visited my GP surgery.

So why wear the T-shirt in the first place?

Here are four reasons why we might be tempted to wear the Victim T-shirt:

Reason 1

You feel you have no other choice. 'That's just the way it is, there's nothing I can do' is the mantra of people who play the victim role. You can adopt a fatalistic approach to life and to the inevitability of being the victim.

Reason 2

Low self-esteem and poor self-image. Either of these factors can distort your view of a situation. Your esteem and self-image can be affected by 'life events' and you are more vulnerable to seeing them damaged when you have experienced a major change such as a divorce, redundancy or an illness. Such events can knock your self-confidence, which, in turn, affects how you think and feel about yourself.

Reason 3

It's become a habit. Some people have been putting on the T-shirt so regularly that they now wear it without even being conscious of the fact. Their wardrobe consists of a whole range of styles and colours of Victim T-shirts – one to suit any occasion.

Reason 4

People actually enjoy wearing it. My research reveals that wearing the Victim T-shirt can bring people many perceived benefits:

- People feel sorry for you and give you more attention.
- It can increase your own feeling of self-importance.
- It is a good excuse for not being able to achieve other things (I would have been able to achieve X if only Y had been more supportive).

- And finally, a very common reason why people wear the Victim T-shirt is simply this: Blaming others frees you from the responsibility of taking charge of your own life.

It's not easy to admit that you have worn the T-shirt. Maybe you haven't; but if you have, what has been your reason? Can you identify people you know who wear the T-shirt? What, in your view, motivates them to wear one?

Points to Ponder...

THE PERSONAL STUFF

When I became ill with chronic fatigue syndrome I went from a high-flying management position to invalidity benefit. Life did not seem very fair and, for a while, I wore the Victim T-shirt. I used to queue up to collect my benefit on the same day pensioners got theirs. I was twenty-four years old. Talking about the weather and the price of baked beans became part of my everyday conversation and did little to make me feel better about myself. I eventually decided that I needed to excuse myself from the pity party and focus on what was still good about my life. I was surprised how much I found. For instance, I realized what an incredible wife I had and how fortunate I was to have so many supportive friends. We still had our own home and I found time to join a creative writing group. We even managed the occasional weekend away, courtesy of someone else's generosity.

People are not always conscious they are wearing the T-shirt. You might not be. So let's explore some characters I have come across on my travels, which may help you spot the signs more clearly.

Victim T-shirt wearers on parade

First let's meet Colin, who is in his early thirties and always has a reason for why he can never remain in a job for longer than three months. He claims he is the victim of office politics; a boss who feels threatened by him, jealousy amongst fellow co-workers and finally, some plot by head office to make his life so unbearable he has no choice other than to resign. Colin is the master of conspiracy theories. On no occasion that I know of has he ever admitted that *he* might have something to do with losing his job.

Dave had been made redundant. He spent months harassing an organization for not appointing him to a position that in his words 'I was clearly right for'. During this time, he failed to apply for any other job until he dealt with what he saw as discrimination. (He did not specify on what grounds he was being discriminated against.) Rather than believe someone else had been more suited to the position, he chose to be the victim. Sometimes people *are* discriminated against and it is right for them to fight for justice. But on other occasions, discrimination is not the reason for people's lack of success – *they* are.

Several months ago I was coaching Lucy, who believed that success was a matter of luck and that she was not lucky. 'It's all about being in the right place at the right time,' she protested, 'and I never am.' Rather than identify and develop her skills and abilities, she chose to believe that life would only get better when she got her big break. Her 'victim mentality' verged on paranoia when she even blamed her accent. 'People think I'm posh and are threatened by me... particularly northerners.' (As a northerner myself I had to smile at such a comment.)

Finally Brian, an office worker I met on one of my courses, seemed to be full of regrets. 'I could really have made something of my life if it had not been for my elderly mother. She has been ill for over 20 years and I have had to look after her. Opportunities have passed me by, including marriage. But what else could I do?' Well, what could he have done? Perhaps if he had seen himself as less of a victim of his domestic circumstances, his life could have been very different. Having a sick or elderly mother does not automatically require a person to remain single. Brian thought it did.

SUMO wisdom

Taking personal responsibility frees you from the trap of blaming, complaining and resenting.

Points to Ponder...

Where are you most likely to wear the Victim T-shirt – at home or at work?

The consequences of wearing the Victim T-shirt

What do Colin, Dave, Lucy and Brian have in common? Simple – wearing the Victim T-shirt has consequences for your life. For them, these include:

- A failure to fulfil their potential.
- Missing out on opportunities because they were too busy feeling sorry for themselves to spot them.
- Other people failing to benefit from their talents.
- Feelings of regret because of what might have been.
- Stagnating, rather than growing as people.

Also their stories indicate the formula on which their lives are built. Sadly it's not $E + R = O$ but $E = O$. They have all failed to realize that it's not just the event but their response that has influenced their outcome. If Colin, Dave, Lucy and Brian changed their response they'd also change their outcome. That's, of course, if they wanted to.

Remember, some people enjoy wearing the Victim T-shirt.

Points to Ponder...

You may have worn the Victim T-shirt regularly, or just on the odd occasion. But when you have, what have been the consequences both to you and those around you? What about the people you know who wear one? What has happened in their lives as a result?

> **SUMO wisdom**
>
> *Your choices are significant. What you do affects who you are and where you end up.*

Having explored the consequences of wearing the Victim T-shirt, you may decide you want to stop wearing one. I want to examine why changing it can be difficult. There are three reasons.

Removing your T-shirt means changing your status quo.

You and I are creatures of habit. Living a life where we do not take responsibility for our actions and where we can blame others for our circumstances is convenient. It becomes a part of our normal way of living. It's what we are familiar with. To change means to move out of our self-created comfort zone. To some people, that is neither appealing nor easy to do.

> **SUMO wisdom**
>
> *When you wear the victim T-shirt, you become a passenger in your life and allow circumstances and other people to determine your direction.*

Removing your T-shirt means going against the current fashion

In the past, when people had accidents, we saw it as part of everyday life and most people were usually prepared to accept some, if not all, the responsibility. Not anymore. Our minds are bombarded with messages such as 'Where there's blame, there's a claim' (and in some cases that is appropriate). But we are now encouraged by some parts of society to feel like victims who are powerless to help ourselves. Blame your teachers, blame your parents, blame the government. Blame anyone but yourself.

We are told we are victims of stress, long hours and unsafe food. Seeds of victim mentality are sown when we are asked questions such as 'Have you felt stressed in the last month?' or 'Have you ever experienced bullying at work?' (Clearly some people do genuinely face such challenging situations, but tackling the problem whilst wearing a Victim T-shirt will not help.)

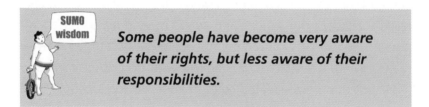

SUMO wisdom *Some people have become very aware of their rights, but less aware of their responsibilities.*

Removing your T-shirt requires courage

It can be uncomfortable to admit to yourself that you have been wearing a Victim T-shirt. This is even harder to do if you feel you are a genuine victim.

So let me be clear. *I do believe* there are innocent victims in life who could justifiably wear the T-shirt. However, some genuine victims choose not to. They decide not to allow events or circumstances to define their identity. Why? Without exception, the people I have met who have been able to move on have done so because they hold on to the following belief:

I am not always responsible for what happens to me, but I am responsible for how I choose to respond.

In March 1993 my wife Helen and I went out for our regular Saturday morning shop. My desire to be back to watch a football programme meant we left town earlier than Helen would have hoped. As we drove out of the town centre a bomb exploded. It killed two young children. Helen, who was eight months pregnant at the time, had walked past the bin where the bomb was planted minutes before it detonated. Those families who lost their sons that day were genuine innocent victims. I met the father of one of those children recently. Remarkably, he seemed to possess no enduring bitterness and appeared to adopt the following attitude.

THE PERSONAL STUFF

Even if you are a genuine victim, ultimately you need to learn how to become a survivor.

On a lighter note, during one of my presentations, I produced a large yellow T-shirt with the word *Victim* emblazoned across the front. I was making the point that we need to get rid of this type of T-shirt. At the end of my talk a man approached me wondering if I sold Victim T-shirts. He knew plenty of people where he worked who he could sell them to.

In case you are wondering, I don't sell Victim T-shirts.

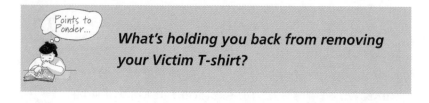

Points to Ponder...

What's holding you back from removing your Victim T-shirt?

So we know some of the reasons why we wear the T-shirt and why it can be difficult to change. But if you want to change it, *how* do you go about it?

How to change your T-shirt

First of all you must decide you want to. Then you need to choose a new one with a different message. The message I suggest is *SUMO*. When you wear this T-shirt, you are deciding to Shut Up being a victim and Move On to taking responsibility. If you want things to be different in your life, you have to make different choices and take different actions. The rest of the book will show you how to do this, but you can make an immediate start by learning to 'mind your language'. It's important that we remove victim language from what we say and what we think and replace it with SUMO sayings. Let me give you some examples. You can come up with your own suggestions for the last one.

Victim language	Replace with SUMO language
Life is not fair	I am unhappy about that, what can I do?
This is just the way I am	How can I improve?
There's nothing I can do	There's always something I can do
It's impossible	Let's find a way
Who is to blame?	How can we move forward?
I am a victim	I am a survivor
What's the point?	_____

As I review the list, I admit that my language has not always been overflowing with SUMO sayings. In the past I have given up too easily because 'There's nothing I can do'; rather than choose the more empowering statement 'There's always something I can do'. I have found it interesting how closed my mind has become to exploring further possibilities when I have adopted the attitude 'It's impossible'. As soon as I put on the Victim T-shirt, it's as if the solution-seeking part of my brain goes into temporary shut-down mode. When you wear the T-shirt you stop looking at how to help yourself (you'll find some great antidotes to this when we explore the next principle).

THE PERSONAL STUFF

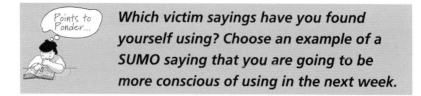

Points to Ponder... **Which victim sayings have you found yourself using? Choose an example of a SUMO saying that you are going to be more conscious of using in the next week.**

In a nutshell

Let me be really clear about what changing your T-shirt does and does not mean. To do so I am going to answer the two most common questions that people pose when we're exploring this topic.

1 Does removing the Victim T-shirt mean I have to accept full responsibility for everything that has happened to me even when it's not my fault? No. Removing the T-shirt simply means you accept responsibility for how you choose to respond to an event. You do not necessarily have to blame yourself for what has happened, but you should accept responsibility for how to move forward.

2 But what if I do believe I have been unfairly treated or discriminated against? Are you suggesting I simply 'get over it' and stop making a fuss? Absolutely and categorically not. The key is not to remain helpless. You may have been a 'victim' but you must see yourself as a survivor. You must assert yourself when necessary and do all you can to challenge inappropriate actions by an individual or organization.

The message from this chapter is that some people, consciously or unconsciously, habitually wear the Victim T-shirt. In doing so, they abdicate responsibility for their lives. Removing the T-shirt is an indication that no matter what life has given us so far or will give us in the future, we take control of our response.

If you want your life to get better, you'll never be able to achieve it until you remove your T-shirt. Change does not happen when circumstances improve; change happens when *you* decide to improve your circumstances.

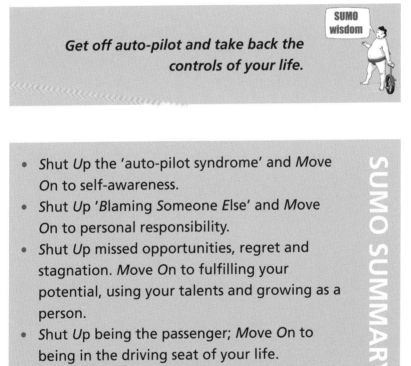

**SUMO
wisdom**

***Get off auto-pilot and take back the
controls of your life.***

- Shut *Up* the 'auto-pilot syndrome' and *Move On* to self-awareness.
- Shut *Up* 'Blaming Someone Else' and *Move On* to personal responsibility.
- Shut *Up* missed opportunities, regret and stagnation. *Move On* to fulfilling your potential, using your talents and growing as a person.
- Shut *Up* being the passenger; *Move On* to being in the driving seat of your life.
- Shut *Up* speaking 'victim' language; *Move On* to speaking SUMO language.
- Shut *Up* wishing your life would get better; *Move On* to making it so.

SUMO SUMMARY

Chapter 3
Develop Fruity Thinking

love quotes. Perhaps my favourite is one I made up (humility always was my strong point). It goes as follows:

'The most important person you will ever talk to is yourself.'

In the previous chapter we explored how we can hinder our lives by talking to ourselves and others in victim language. Talking to yourself (at least silently) is generally referred to as thinking (other phrases you may have heard are self-talk, inner-dialogue or your mindset, but ultimately whatever the language we use, we're exploring the conversations that go on inside our heads). In this next SUMO principle we are going to explore how we think. Thinking is a little like breathing – most of the time we are not aware we are doing it. People do not wake up in the morning and say, 'I think I will breathe today', and likewise, neither do they pay much attention to how they think.

So why is it so important? What is the connection between my thinking and the results I am experiencing in my life? The answer lies in the fact that the way we think, i.e. talk to ourselves in our heads, significantly impacts upon what we do in our actions, and it is our actions that determine the results we achieve in life.

The TEAR model

Imagine you have been asked by a work colleague to make a presentation to their department about the work you do. Your immediate thought is, 'I hate making presentations, I always go to pieces'. You feel intimidated by the prospect and decline the request by stating you have too many other commitments at present. The result? You still fear presentations and you miss out on the opportunity of helping a colleague. You just went through the TEAR process:

*T*hinking → *E*motions (or feelings) → *A*ctions (or behaviour) → *R*esults (or outcomes)

Another way to illustrate this is as follows:

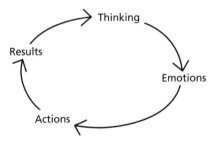

Life can become a self-fulfilling prophecy.

William James, one of the pioneers of modern psychology, said, 'You can change your life by changing your attitude'. Quite simply, when you *think* differently, you *feel* differently, *behave* differently and ultimately *achieve* different results. Suppose when you were asked to do the presentation, you thought, 'I'll give it a try... they wouldn't have asked me if they didn't feel I could do it'. You might not feel confident, but neither are you gripped by fear. You take action by preparing and then delivering your presentation. You get a different result and outcome because you changed how you thought about the situation.

SUMO wisdom *Reflecting on how we think is one of the most powerful ways we can take control over our lives.*

Points to Ponder... *Think of a situation or challenging experience that you have faced. Record some of your thoughts (the conversations inside your head) below.*

How were you feeling at the time – anxious, fearful, confident, excited, daunted, motivated?

What actions did you take? Did you avoid taking certain actions?

What were your results? What was the outcome?

In what ways would your outcome have been different if you had changed your thinking?

How might the formula E + R = O have helped in this situation?

What influences your thinking?

How you view your life, yourself and other people is influenced by many factors. Let us examine four of them.

1 Your background influences your thinking

A leading British entrepreneur records in his biography how, as a youngster, his mother would often tell him the following: 'Dare to be different'; 'Be prepared to rock the boat'; 'It's OK to make mistakes as long as you learn from them'; 'Life is not a rehearsal'; 'Never forget – no one is any better or worse than you'. Brought up in that environment, it is not surprising that this person became a risk taker, a visionary leader and a person who, despite setbacks, always bounced back. Contrast that with a delegate on my course who told me recently that his father's advice on how to succeed in life was, 'Always wear navy and keep a low profile'.

Now that would be funny if it wasn't so sad. You see, the main message that person received was this: 'Blend in. Play small. Don't take risks.'

The most important message you receive as you grow up is the one that influences how you see yourself. Messages that affirm you for who you are, as opposed to for what you do, will help you develop a healthy sense of personal identity. Equally, a bombardment of messages that remind you of your inadequacies and failings will help sow the seeds of low self-esteem.

> **SUMO wisdom**
>
> *Be careful what you say to children.*
> *If they hear it often enough, they*
> *begin to believe it.*

2 Your previous experiences influence your thinking

Have you ever had to give a talk in public? Imagine (if you need to) that you have, and your input was such that most of the audience were cured of their insomnia. It would be understandable if you did not rush to do another one.

Or maybe when you took a risk or tried something different, you did not get the outcome you were expecting. It is likely that you will be more cautious in the future. Perhaps the last time you went to a restaurant you received excellent service and you are eager to return. *Whatever your previous experiences have been, they influence your attitude and your expectations.* This also relates to when we meet people, and is why aiming to create a positive first impression is so important. Our brief encounters with people can create attitudes that last a lifetime.

3 The company you keep influences your thinking

The 1970s British comedy series *Dad's Army* starred a Scottish character called Frazer. When not in the Home Guard, he worked in a funeral parlour. It suited his personality. Whenever there was a set of circumstances or a situation that could be described as challenging, Frazer would cry, 'We're dooooooomed!' Watching Frazer was amusing, but working with a 'Frazer-type character' is not. Someone who exaggerates problems and can always pinpoint the negative in a situation does not help cultivate a positive way of thinking in those around them.

SUMO wisdom

Beware of BMWs. People who spend their lives Bitching, Moaning and Whinging.

4 The media influence your thinking

What have you read in the last week? A newspaper? A magazine? Which television programmes have you watched, or radio shows have you listened to? Although we may watch a programme or read a magazine purely for entertainment, or in order to 'chill out', continual exposure to the media subtly influences our outlook on life.

Without the media, where would fashion be? Where would celebrities be? Where would politics be? There is nothing inherently wrong with the media, but we need to be aware of how it shapes our thinking, particularly in relation to how we see ourselves. The obsession in some parts of the media with the appearance of supermodels and celebrities can cause young people in particular to feel dissatisfied with their own appearance and can affect what they think of themselves.

It can also give us a distorted view of life. Fear is a great marketing tool. A scare story gets our attention. Good news rarely does. So what makes the news? The rare, the vivid, the catastrophic. And you wonder why, when in the developed world our chances of living a longer, healthier, safer life are greater than any time in human history, anxiety and stress amongst people are increasing at an alarming rate.

While I was working with a group of people who had been made redundant, I explained how their view that 'there are no jobs' was a distorted one. I showed them a regional newspaper I had been reading that included a story on its *front page* about a pensioner who dropped a frozen turkey on her foot. Fortunately, after her foot was X-rayed she was given the all clear by the hospital and discharged. Tucked away in the same paper on page three was a story about 800 new jobs being created in the area. I then showed them another paper where the news of a factory closing down was on the front page. These people's view of the job market was influenced by what the media chose to highlight. Negative news and mindless trivia dominated the front pages. The positive stories were harder to find.

THE PERSONAL STUFF

So our thoughts, beliefs and attitudes are influenced by several factors. They shape our lives whether we are aware of them or not. The key to all this is self-awareness. However, whilst it is important to recognize the influence of various external factors, be careful you don't start to slip on the Victim T-shirt, i.e. 'I think negatively because of how my parents brought me up', or 'My wife insists we watch medical dramas where there's never a happy ending'. We still need to take personal responsibility for our thinking despite those external influences. Remember E + R = O.

Consider how your upbringing and background have influenced how you see yourself. What messages about yourself do you remember hearing as a child? Were they mainly positive or negative ones? Think about your circle of friends. How do they influence your thinking? Do you know any BMWs? (People who bitch, moan and whinge.) How do they affect you?

Be aware when you next read a paper, go online or watch a television programme how the media are influencing your view of the world.

We highlighted earlier, through the TEAR model (*T*hinking, *E*motions, *A*ctions, *R*esults) the importance of our thinking. Let's examine in more detail how certain types of thinking patterns can hinder our ability to be successful. I refer to these thinking patterns as 'faulty thinking'.

Four types of faulty thinking

The first type of faulty thinking... the Inner Critic

This is the voice inside your head that highlights your weaknesses and undermines your confidence. It is not the voice of encouragement to do better, it is the voice of condemnation. You make a mistake on Tuesday and ten days (or ten years) later you are still beating yourself up about it. The need to *S*hut *U*p criticizing yourself is great, but people fail to *M*ove *O*n. In extreme cases, you are beating yourself up about events and actions that happened years ago. Driven perhaps by the mistaken belief that 'I must be perfect', or 'It is wrong to make mistakes', the Inner Critic can help demolish your fragile walls of confidence.

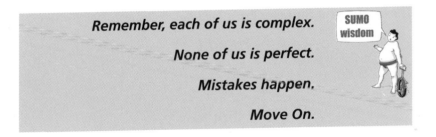

Remember, each of us is complex.

None of us is perfect.

Mistakes happen.

Move On.

The Inner Critic takes root in our lives from early childhood, and is fed and watered by the four factors we have just explored:

1   Your personal background
2   Your previous experiences
3   The company you keep
4   The media.

THE PERSONAL STUFF

I recently worked in a local school with a group of 11–12-year-olds. I started to explore the 'Inner Critic' with them and help them to understand its destructive nature. In order to tackle it, I suggested that we needed to expose it. I split them up into small groups and asked them to write a list of sayings that they might hear from the Inner Critic. Deep down, I hoped they would struggle to come up with many. Within five minutes, they were asking for more paper.

The language of the Inner Critic includes:

'I ought...'

'I must...'

'I should...'

'I'm always getting it wrong.'

'How could I have been so stupid?'

Sometimes the voice of the Inner Critic speaks as an internal third party. These are phrases I have regularly heard inside my own head:

'Why didn't you... ?'

'That's typical of you.'

'You always get that wrong.'

'Don't get ideas above your station.'

'Do you honestly think people will want to hear that?'

The emotional intensity behind what you say to yourself determines whether the impact of the Inner Critic is that of a common cold (annoying but not life-threatening) or pneumonia (much more serious with potentially damaging consequences).

SUMO wisdom

It's not simply what you say to yourself that matters. It's how you say it and how much you believe it that counts.

However, this next point is crucial.

Silencing the Inner Critic is not an abdication of your desire to improve or an abandonment of responsibility regarding a mistake made. Your ultimate goal is to become a coach to yourself and not allow past mistakes to make a prisoner of your potential.

We still need to have conversations with ourselves, but the voice we need to listen to is that of the *Inner Coach*. This voice has your best interests at heart. It is *for* you. The Inner Critic condemns you. The Inner Coach encourages you and inspires you to improve, and in a few pages' time you will learn how to tune in to this voice.

My Inner Critic raises its head when I've made a mistake. It's skilled at allowing me to spend days, even weeks beating myself up over some things that were genuine mistakes. Some years ago I was best man at a wedding. Before the meal I, along with the bridal party, lined up to greet the guests before they sat down to eat. I noticed one woman wearing a maternity dress who looked like she was due to give birth in the very near future. My suspicions were confirmed when the groom commented, 'Not long to your big day then?' 'No, only three weeks,' she replied, 'and I can hardly wait.' When it was my turn to meet her I made momentary eye contact then looked at her bump and enquired, 'What are you hoping for, a boy or a girl?' The silence was

THE PERSONAL STUFF

deafening. Then she leaned forward and replied, 'I get married in three weeks and I am not pregnant.' Cue the Inner Critic. I found it hard to forgive myself for causing such embarrassment. But I learned my lesson. I am so mindful now that even if I am in a maternity ward, I would be hesitant to make any comments – and with good reason. A friend of mine who knew a neighbour was due to give birth imminently, asked her, 'When are you due?' She replied, 'I gave birth two weeks ago.'

Points to Ponder...

Do you suffer from the Inner Critic? What phrases do you find your Inner Critic saying to you? In what situations do you find the Inner Critic speaks loudest? Does it happen more at work or at home?

The second type of faulty thinking... the Broken Record

When we get stuck in a groove of thinking, we continually replay the same messages within our heads. You could be in 'Broken Record Inner Critic' mode whereby you continually analyse and criticize your behaviour. Alternatively, you might simply keep on talking to anyone and everyone about your unhappiness and dissatisfaction with your job, a person or a situation. Stuck in this way of thinking, you churn over your thoughts but take no action to resolve your problem.

Some people fall into an irrational way of thinking whereby they believe that by moaning about a situation it will somehow improve things.

It won't.

But it will make you feel more miserable.

> **SUMO wisdom**
>
> *There may be times when the problems of your past don't need to be fixed or sorted – they need to be left behind.*

> **Points to Ponder**
>
> *What do you tend to moan about? Why? How long does your moaning last? Does it make you feel better? What effect does it have on you and other people?*

The third type of faulty thinking... the Martyr Syndrome

I know martyrs can be viewed as heroic and their actions taken as a sacrifice for a worthy cause. But when I use the term in this context I mean the sort of thinking that says the following:

'I am unworthy.'

'I must sacrifice my needs to serve others.'

'I don't deserve to be happy.'

'My views are less important than other people's.'

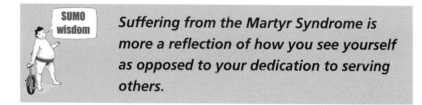

Suffering from the Martyr Syndrome is more a reflection of how you see yourself as opposed to your dedication to serving others.

The reasons for suffering this type of thinking have been covered in the previous chapter, 'Change Your T-shirt'. However, one cause we have yet to mention is why martyrs wear 'Victim T-shirts'.

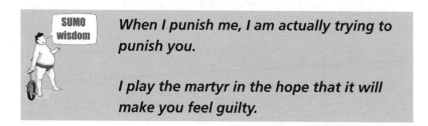

When I punish me, I am actually trying to punish you.

I play the martyr in the hope that it will make you feel guilty.

When you try and help a martyr who has been complaining about how unfair life is, and how it is always them that has the 'short end of the stick', they often refuse. It is difficult to continue playing the martyr when you accept help from others. The truth is, some people are actually at their happiest when they've got something to be miserable about. Sad, but true.

When have you played the martyr? Does it happen most with family and friends or bosses and colleagues? When did you last ask for some help?

The fourth type of faulty thinking… Trivial Pursuits

Another way of understanding this type of thinking is when we make mountains out of molehills (although we'll see in our final chapter when this is appropriate). People have the ability to get angry or upset over the most trivial issues. Relationships are ruined and people suffer from anxiety, often not because of something major, but due to something insignificant. Trivial Pursuits can have a snowball effect and completely distort your view of reality.

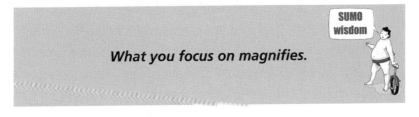

SUMO wisdom

What you focus on magnifies.

This inability to see things in perspective can result in a reaction or outburst that is completely disproportionate to the actual event. Sound familiar? It does to me.

This type of thinking can be closely allied to the others. You can be a 'Broken Record Inner Critic' about something quite trivial. And we may play the martyr because of some insignificant event.

For example, let us say that at work some information was not passed on to you, and although it was of little relevance, your response is, 'No one ever tells me anything around here, I'm always the last to know'. Now this next point is really important. So much so, I want you to read it twice and make sure you digest its significance.

Your emotional energy can be exhausted due to trivial pursuits and your focus can be distracted from the really important issues in your life.

SUMO wisdom

Perhaps it's not the circumstances that need to change, but more your perspective of those circumstances.

Points to Ponder...

What are some of the trivial issues you allow yourself to get upset over? What are the consequences of your reaction? When do you get into Trivial Pursuits? At work? In the car? With your children? With your partner? Here's a brief exercise to identify where and how often you're in Faulty Thinking. Be as honest as you can with your answers.

	Daily	2–3 times a week	Occasionally	Hardly ever
	At home/ At work	At home/ At work	At home/ At work	At home/ At work
Inner Critic	☐☐	☐☐	☐☐	☐☐
Broken Record	☐☐	☐☐	☐☐	☐☐
Martyr Syndrome	☐☐	☐☐	☐☐	☐☐
Trivial Pursuits	☐☐	☐☐	☐☐	☐☐

Now most people just scanned through the exercise and didn't complete it. Remember, the value of this book is not just what you read, but your engagement with the exercises. So if you've moved on from the exercise without completing it, I challenge you to go back and complete it. It won't take you long, but its insights for you could be helpful.

For instance, I'm aware I experience faulty thinking far more in my home life than I do at work.

So it will be interesting, having completed the above, to see if you experience one or two types of faulty thinking more than others. You will also find it enlightening to see the context in which you experience the faulty thinking. Why don't you put in your diary, say three months from now, a follow-up action to revisit this exercise and see what changes there have been.

I recently worked with an organization on a 'Succeeding Through Change' programme for managers and staff. What fascinated me was what constituted 'massive change' for some staff. One guy said, 'They've only gone and moved my desk' (it was still in the same office). Others complained that the coffee machine had moved to a different floor and they now had to climb the stairs in order to get a drink. From my own experience, I have been close to declaring war due to the fact that I often find toothbrushes in every room of the house except the bathroom.

THE PERSONAL STUFF

Why slip into faulty thinking?

At times we all slip into faulty thinking and often for quite irrational reasons. So why do we do it? In the chapter E + R = O we explored three reasons why we respond the way we do to certain situations. Here's a reminder of what they were:

Habits
Conditioning
Emotions

All three could be reasons why we slip into faulty thinking. It could simply be habitual. Secondly, we've been conditioned to think in a certain way. Finally, our emotional state can influence our thinking. But there's a fourth reason:

Fatigue

Mental or physical exhaustion can lead to us being unable to think in a way that is helpful and constructive. So it's worth being aware that there are a number of factors conspiring against us developing Fruity Thinking and causing us to slip into Faulty Thinking.

Now, in this next section I'd like to explore with you how your brain works (in a simplified way). This will, in turn, provide further understanding and awareness as to how we think and how that impacts upon our behaviour.

How the brain works

If we were to take a cross-sectional view of your brain, we could divide it into three distinct sections.

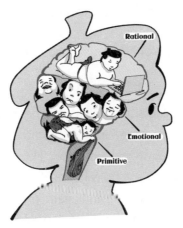

1 **Rational brain.** Sometimes referred to as the neo cortex or 'higher brain'.
2 **Emotional brain.** This is part of the limbic system and is sometimes referred to as the 'mid-brain'.
3 **Primitive brain.** Also known as the reptilian brain or 'lower brain', it controls our fight or flight response, our desire for food and our sex drive.

So when we are feeling tired, hungry, anxious or threatened, we are not feeling particularly rational. In the heat of the moment, we may lash out physically or verbally, or run away from a situation in a state of panic. This is our fight or flight response. We react to a situation without first thinking through our response. (This might explain the scenes in my household when I can't find my toothbrush.)

The upside of the primitive and emotional brain

However, to be driven by our emotional or primitive brain is not necessarily wrong; it is part of who we are as human beings. If everyone were completely rational about things in life, our world would lack passion, variety and excitement.

Appreciating the highs only happens because we have experienced the lows.

And being rational can sometimes be dangerous. If you are in a meeting room and a man-eating lion (which also has a taste for women) walks in, the rational response: 'How did that get in here and why isn't it wearing a visitor's badge?' will do little to save you. When it comes to matters of life and death, primitive brain wins every time. We don't have time to be rational; we must react instinctively.

Our emotional brain helps us to appreciate art, to be passionate about something and to engage creatively in an idea. People are moved to take action over an issue, not due to some rational urge, but because emotionally they feel compelled to do so.

The upside of the rational brain

But here's the reality. Some of the problems and challenges we face in life are due to our inability to tap into our rational brain. You see, being rational can bring a fresh perspective and new insights to an issue. It helps us to utilize the problem-solving attributes of our higher brain. It can prevent us over-reacting to an event, and avoid saying and doing something that we later regret. By accessing our rational brain, we can discover an antidote to faulty thinking, and that's a process I call 'Developing Fruity Thinking'.

So how can we engage our rational brain?

The key to engaging your rational brain is to ask yourself questions. Questions are powerful. The quality of them determines the quality of your answers. To understand this more fully, let's explore for a moment how our amazing brain works.

The influence of your RAS

Your RAS (Reticular Activating System) is a part of your brain that filters information. Our brains are being continually bombarded with thousands of pieces of information from the environment around us. If we were to consciously take note of them all, we would experience brain overload. So your RAS acts like a filter and helps you to 'notice' information that is relevant, important, of interest or perhaps unusual.

I do a great deal of driving. Ask me which car is the most popular on the road and I would not be able to tell you. However, when I was thinking of getting myself a different type of car, I suddenly noticed that car everywhere. When my wife became pregnant, we immediately noticed how many other women were expecting babies. (Although because of my previous experience I couldn't always be sure and I certainly wouldn't ask when they were due.)

When we are experiencing faulty thinking, our brains seek out information to support what we are thinking. If we believe we are always failing, then our RAS spots examples to reinforce that belief. Interestingly, it also ignores the evidence that we were not looking for. For example, asking me to count how many BMW cars I see on the motorway means I ignore and fail to notice other makes of car.

Equally, when I am looking for my failures, I ignore my successes. Questions such as 'Why am I so unlucky?' or 'Why does this always happen to me?' tune your RAS to seek out information as to why you are not succeeding.

But when you change the question, you change your focus. Your RAS starts to notice 'things' it had previously been ignoring. So let's explore how to re-tune our RAS and tap into the benefits of using our rational brain.

The following seven questions have provided me with a way of moving on from the Faulty Thinking of the Inner Critic, the Broken Record, the Martyr Syndrome and Trivial Pursuits and into Fruity Thinking. They are the questions I use when I'm listening to the Inner Coach. With each question I have included its underlying message.

1 *Where is this issue on a scale of 1–10? (where 10 = death)*
   Decide what is really important.
2 *How important will this be in six months' time?*
   See the big picture. Get things in perspective.
3 *Is my response appropriate and effective?*
   You choose your response.
4 *How can I influence or improve the situation?*
   Identify your own resources to bring about change.
5 *What can I learn from this?*
   Look for the learning in everything – even setbacks.
6 *What will I do differently next time?*
   Learning brings change.
7 *What can I find that's positive in this situation?*
   Searching for the positive opens our minds to new possibilities.

There is nothing remarkable about the questions, but it is the answers they lead to that can help us succeed. They have become part of my 'life tool kit' and one of the strategies I use to help me tackle various challenges and situations that I regularly face. (You can download a copy of the seven questions by visiting www .theSUMOguy.com/downloads.aspx.)

> **SUMO wisdom**
>
> *If you are not happy with the answers life is giving you, then ask some different questions.*

So let's explore the importance of each question. The first three questions are designed to help you Shut Up. To Shut Up means to pause, to reflect and to listen. It means get off auto-pilot and stop reacting to a situation like you always do. They are designed to provide perspective. When we are in emotional and primitive brain we tend to lose perspective.

1 Where is this issue on a scale of 1–10?

I am often asked what I mean by the scale of 1–10. For me, 1 on the scale means something insignificant and minor, whereas 10 represents a major issue, such as death, for example. Your scale is determined by your values. A scratch on my car is definitely a below-5 event, whereas I appreciate for some people it is close to being a 10! Sometimes in the immediacy of the moment, I react to an event as if it is a 9; yet this question can quickly remind me it may only be a 2.

2 How important will this be in six months' time?

This is very similar to the first question. Again it is asking us to put things into perspective. It can serve as a reminder that what we are allowing to cause us great stress at the moment could actually be forgotten in six months' time. (Stop reading for a moment. Cast your mind back six months. Can you remember what was causing you stress at the time? Probably not, eh?) Is your issue something you may struggle to recall six months from now? If not, fine, but at least you are gaining some perspective.

3 Is my response appropriate and effective?

What a great question to ask ourselves. This question allows you to consider whether or not your response will ultimately help or hinder the situation. A knee-jerk reaction that might seem reasonable at the time may seem very different a few hours or even a few minutes later.

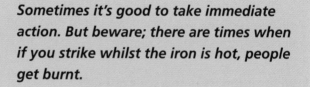

SUMO wisdom *Sometimes it's good to take immediate action. But beware; there are times when if you strike whilst the iron is hot, people get burnt.*

The next four questions are designed to help us to 'Move On' and to focus on how to achieve a different outcome.

4 How can I influence or improve the situation?

When we are under stress, our emotions have a habit of hijacking the problem-solving skills within our higher brain. Asking ourselves this question immediately helps us to focus on how we can resolve the situation. It helps us *Shut Up* blaming circumstances and people for our situation and to *Move On* to identifying ways we can help ourselves. Remember that learning to help ourselves may still involve the support of other people.

I once ran a workshop on interviewing skills for a group of office staff who were about to be made redundant. One woman remarked, 'I'll go to pieces if they ask me what my weaknesses are. I hate that question and just pray I'm not asked it.' 'What if they do?' I replied. 'Well, fingers crossed they don't or I'm in trouble.'

Hope is not a strategy. This woman clearly thought it was. By the end of the course, we had focused on what answers she could give if asked about her weaknesses. Common sense I know – but not always common practice.

THE PERSONAL STUFF

5 What can I learn from this?

Life is always trying to teach us things. A great many people I talk with relate to having spent time beating themselves up over a mistake they've made. I have found a great antidote to my Inner Critic is this question. Rather than send myself on a guilt trip, can I use whatever has happened as an opportunity to learn?

6 What will I do differently next time?

If I repeat the same mistake, then I have not actually learnt anything. Real learning brings about change. Learn from it. Make changes. Move on.

7 What can I find that's positive in this situation?

In my work as a speaker, I realize this: sometimes it is not new ideas that people crave, it is the inspiration to implement the ideas they have. This question moves us away from what is wrong in a situation and directs our attention to what we can find that is positive. When we do so, we may identify possibilities we failed to see previously. We need inspiration to move forward. This question can provide it.

Points to Ponder...

Now it's your turn. Let's go through the seven questions, only this time have a particular issue or challenge in mind as we work through them. There's some space to record your thoughts and actions, and I've included some additional thoughts with each question.

1 **Where is this issue on a scale of 1–10? (Where 10 = death)**

Put a mark on the scale below:

1   2   3   4   5   6   7   8   9   10

2 **How important will this be in six months' time?**

(If you were to revisit question 1 six months from now would the issue have moved up or down the scale?)

3 *Is my response appropriate and effective?*

(Are you in primitive, emotional or rational brain at the moment regarding the situation? Your current response may feel appropriate, but in terms of E + R = O how effective is your response in terms of helping you achieve a more favourable outcome?)

4 *How can I influence or improve the situation?*

(Write down some possible actions you could take to influence and improve the situation. Who could help you? What skills and abilities do you already have that could help you right now? What's the first action you can take?)

Who could help –

Your existing skills and abilities –

First action to take –

5 *What can I learn from this?*
(What have you learnt about yourself and other people? If you had to list your top three lessons from this current experience, what would they be?)

1

2

3

6 *What will I do differently next time?*

(Be careful not to dwell on the possible failings in this situation, but move on to future focus and what response you will make in the future to achieve a more favourable outcome.)

7 *What can I find that's positive in this situation?*

(Make a list of at least three positives you can take from your current situation.)

1

2

3

THE PERSONAL STUFF

A couple of years ago, a potential new client e-mailed me. I had been recommended to them as someone who could speak to their staff on the subject of motivation. This was a high-profile organization with an international reputation. To gain such a prestigious client would be a real coup for my business. We spoke on the phone and successfully agreed fees, dates and the content of my presentation. It only remained for some minor details to be ironed out before the event. I was thrilled. A few days later, having not received the confirmation promised, I e-mailed them a reminder. They replied instantly. It was not the news I wanted to hear. 'Due to circumstances, we are no longer able to proceed, but can I thank you for your interest in working with our organization.' I was fuming and felt tempted to put on my Victim T-shirt. In my anger and disappointment, I immediately set about responding to their e-mail. There were a number of issues I wanted to address.

1 How long had they known they no longer required my services? I had held the agreed date for several days and turned down another opportunity.
2 A phone call rather than hiding behind a vague e-mail would have been appreciated.

3 As for their comment 'thank you for your interest in working with our organization'; well, excuse me, but who contacted whom first?

As I typed the e-mail, I felt an increasing sense of self-satisfaction. I would teach them to let me down in such an unprofessional manner. Then, in mid-sentence, I stopped and thought, *'Is my response appropriate and effective?'* Well, it certainly felt appropriate, but was it going to be effective? If I pressed the 'Send' button, any opportunity of working with the organization in the future would be zero. So what did I do? Pressed delete and then did nothing for twenty-four hours. Then when I re-read their e-mail I thought about the fourth question to help me SUMO.

How can I influence or improve the situation?

My focus changed from feeling like the victim and believing I had been treated unfairly, to tuning in my RAS to identify another way forward. In a calmer, more solution-focused state, I sent my response. Although not sure of the reason why my services were no longer required, I suggested running a lunchtime session for staff for a reduced fee and also gave them further options regarding what other topics I could talk about. Within two hours, they had booked me to speak. They had their speaker and I had a new, prestigious client.

Just as you do not cut the hedge with the lawnmower, so it is also important to recognize that each question is appropriate in some situations but not in others. As you will see in the next chapter, sometimes people are not ready emotionally to ask themselves these questions. They are not a quick-fix magic solution. However, what they can do is cause us to take time to reflect and focus our minds in a more productive way.

SUMO wisdom

The quality of the solution can depend on the quality of the question.

Points to Ponder...

Which of the seven questions were most useful in helping you work through your issue? Choose two questions you want to be more conscious of using in the next few weeks.

In a nutshell

Faulty thinking is often based on the following false beliefs:

- *Inner Critic:* 'I lack value. My only worth comes through my performance and what other people think of me. When I fail to reach a particular standard I must punish myself.'
- *Broken Record:* 'Talking and thinking about something for long enough is an adequate substitute for taking action.'
- *Martyr Syndrome:* 'Life is what happens to me. I am not responsible for what happens; fate, luck and other people determine my destiny.'
- *Trivial Pursuits:* 'Urgency determines importance. That is how to prioritize. Ignore the big picture.'

The antidote to faulty thinking is Fruity Thinking. It comes when we listen to our Inner Coach and take a conscious grip of our thoughts. Fruity Thinking is based on the following beliefs:

- I am of worth because of who I am, not because of what I do.
- I learn from the past but I do not remain rooted in it. I know when to let go and when to move on.
- I am responsible. I have choices. No one else plays as big a role in determining my destiny as I do.
- I choose to major on the majors. I am aware of the big picture and focus on what is important. I see things in perspective.

- If you want different results in your life, change your thinking. *Thinking* → *Emotions* → *Actions* → *Results.*
- *Shut Up* the auto-pilot and *Move On* to self-awareness. Our thinking is influenced by our background, previous experience, the company we keep and the media.
- *Shut Up* the Inner Critic and *Move On* to listening to the Inner Coach.
- *Shut Up* being a Broken Record and *Move On* to taking action.
- *Shut Up* the Martyr Syndrome and *Move On* to taking ownership of your life.
- *Shut Up* Trivial Pursuits and *Move On* to majoring on the majors.
- *Shut Up* being overly dominated by your emotional and primitive brain and *Move On* to using your rational brain.
- *Shut Up* immediately reacting and *Move On* to choosing your response.
- *Shut Up* the questions that lead to faulty answers and *Move On* to Fruity Thinking.

Chapter 4

Hippo Time Is OK

R ecently a delegate took me to one side and said, 'Paul, I enjoy what you're saying and I agree with it up to a point. But sometimes it isn't easy to SUMO. Sometimes I'm not ready to move on. Is that wrong?'

You may be thinking the same question. To answer it, let me tell you about my friend Steve.

Steve was recounting how his favourite rugby league team had lost an important cup match. When he returned home his wife, who does not share his passion for rugby, said, 'Never mind, there's always next year.' At the time, this was the last thing Steve wanted to hear. 'I just wanted to wallow, to be left alone and to dwell on what might have been,' he told me.

None of us want to hear some well-meaning person telling us to cheer up when we've just experienced a major setback or disappointment. The fact is, telling someone to SUMO might, in some circumstances, be both insensitive and unhelpful, particularly if what they have experienced is serious and significant.

So what should we do?

When Steve used the term 'wallow', a picture of a hippopotamus wallowing in mud immediately sprang to mind. It was then that I realized that, on occasions, before people can SUMO they may need to wallow – to have, as I call it, some *Hippo Time.* So let's explore when we might need Hippo Time.

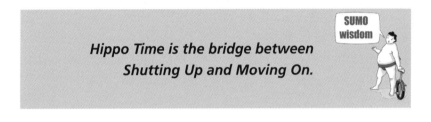

Hippo Time is the bridge between
Shutting Up and Moving On.

When Hippo Time might be necessary

The need for Hippo Time will vary according to the person and their situation. But here are some events that may trigger a period of wallowing (the list is similar to the one we looked at in the E + R = O chapter):

- Your partner dumps you.
- You miss out on that promotion at work.
- You are one number short of a big win on the lottery.
- You miss your train or plane.
- Your sports team loses an important match.
- You fail to get the job you were interviewed for.
- A publisher rejects your latest book proposal.
- An event you were looking forward to is cancelled unexpectedly.
- A friend lets you down in some way.
- You discover your brand new conservatory has a structurally unsafe roof and the company that built it has gone out of business (I'll explain this one later).

- Your organization announces more changes and, as a result, you move departments.
- Your house is broken into.
- You lose or break something of sentimental value.
- You are made redundant.
- You're an England football fan and the game has gone to penalties.

Why not add two of your own events that have led to a legitimate time of wallowing?

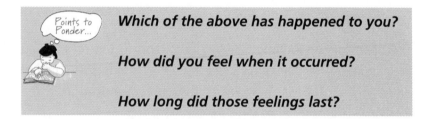

Points to Ponder...

Which of the above has happened to you?

How did you feel when it occurred?

How long did those feelings last?

Why do we need Hippo Time?

To be simply told to *Shut Up, Move On* when any, or if you are really unlucky, all of the above has occurred is to deny reality. As human beings we are, by nature, emotional. A life without experiencing emotional highs and lows would be boring and bland. You are not a robot who can turn your emotions on and off at the flick of a switch. In order to move on, you need, at times, to acknowledge the emotions you are feeling. There will be occasions when, with the help of the seven questions we explored in Chapter 3, we can SUMO in an instant. But let us be real here – there will be other occasions when we need to take a Hippo Time detour.

It's OK to not always feel OK.

Hippo Time provides you with the opportunity to experience your emotional lows and to be honest about those feelings.

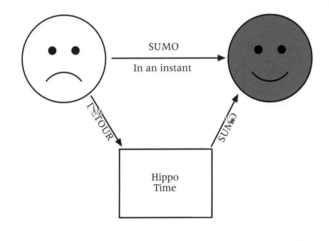

*When you deny the negative, you block
the road to positive recovery.*

Understanding our emotions

Sometimes we can become confused about our emotions. Is it wrong to cry? Should we always be happy? Let's get some clarity about our emotions.

Unhelpful beliefs about emotions	Helpful beliefs about emotions
Showing emotions makes you appear weak	Emotions are part of what makes us human
Men should never express their emotions	Expressing emotions is a release valve for internal pressure
Showing emotions embarrasses other people	No feeling is wrong; it is what we do with the feelings that counts

> **SUMO wisdom**
>
> *Sometimes it's OK to feel mad, bad or sad – in fact it's normal.*

Emotions are valid but they can also create confusion within us. Some people I know actually find value in keeping a 'feelings diary'. Rather than record what they did on a particular day, they record how they felt. Writing down our feelings may help us gain a greater insight into ourselves and also help us notice how our emotions vary from day to day.

Having Hippo Time can be extremely helpful. But it can also be very unproductive. So how can you make the most of Hippo Time? Who is best to help you during this period and who should you avoid? How can you prevent yourself wallowing for too long? Here are some ground rules:

Top three tips for Hippo Time

Tip 1   Be careful who you talk to

The phrase *'a trouble shared is a trouble halved'* is an important principle, but it is not always appropriate. There are people who have the unique ability to make you feel worse after you have spoken to them. I refer to these people as 'Awfulisers'. Their favourite phrase is, unsurprisingly, 'That's awful'.

A friend of mine recalls how, having received a parking ticket, a colleague in his office told him he was the unluckiest person he had ever met. My friend was reminded of all the 'unlucky events' that had occurred to him over the last twelve months (many of which he had forgotten). When his colleague was told the cost of the ticket, the reply came, 'That's awful, just think what you could have done with that money'.

Some people, in seeking to help, encourage you to wear the Victim T-shirt and, metaphorically speaking, they are giving you more mud to wallow in. When you start talking to certain people you have a problem, but it's quickly turning to depression.

Also, avoid people who are only too keen to share advice or their experiences before you have had a chance to vent. They will hijack your Hippo Time to recount all *their* worries and woes. Suddenly your issue becomes their issue – it's now all about them, not you.

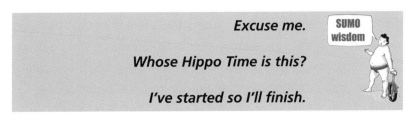

Excuse me.

Whose Hippo Time is this?

I've started so I'll finish.

SUMO wisdom

You may also want to avoid those 'I am positive but I have no grasp of reality' people. You lose your legs in an accident, and they smile sincerely and say, 'At least you've still got your arms'. Or you split up with your partner and they say 'There's plenty more fish in the sea'.

You need to find someone who is prepared to actively listen, who allows you to talk and who doesn't feel obliged to offer advice. And it can be a challenge to find such a person.

Points to Ponder...

Who would you identify as the most appropriate person to have your Hippo Time with? Who would you avoid? Or do you prefer to have Hippo Time on your own?

Tip 2 Be careful how many people you talk to

Our temptation when asked the question, 'How are you?' or, 'How was your weekend?' is to answer honestly and comprehensively. After all, if I'm in Hippo Time and someone asks the question, I'm entitled to give them an answer. Right? Wrong. There are two reasons why you have to be discerning about how many people you tell your troubles to.

Firstly, the more times you tell your story, the more you replay and re-live the negative experience and emotions associated with it. Distracted perhaps by a particular task or activity, you may actually feel fine until a colleague or neighbour enquires how you are.

In that moment you have a choice. I am not suggesting that you 'put on a brave face' and deny that you are in Hippo Time. However, the question is this: does this person really want to know how you are, or are they simply making polite conversation? If it is the latter, give them your ten-second version of your story. If it is the former, then you may choose to tell the longer version, but only if you feel you want to.

This piece of SUMO wisdom is so important to remember:

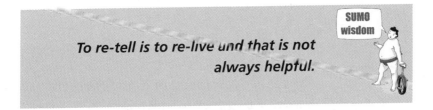

SUMO wisdom

To re-tell is to re-live and that is not always helpful.

Secondly – how can I put this nicely? Actually, I can't. So here goes: in my experience, around 80% of people who ask you how you are, are not particularly interested in your answer. Not only can it be unhelpful to go into replay mode about your troubles, but you may also be labelled a bore. So, for everyone's sake, beware how many people you share your Hippo Time with.

Points to Ponder...

Who would be the people you typically off-load your troubles to? Are you possibly telling too many people?

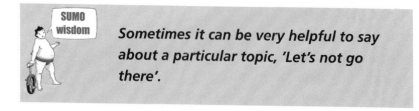

SUMO wisdom

Sometimes it can be very helpful to say about a particular topic, 'Let's not go there'.

Tip 3 Be careful how long your Hippo Time lasts

Some people can get used to wallowing in the mud. You may have been encouraged to lengthen your stay due to the attention you receive and wallowing can feel comfortable and comforting. But ultimately, spending too long in the mud of self-pity becomes unhelpful.

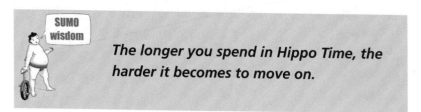

SUMO wisdom

The longer you spend in Hippo Time, the harder it becomes to move on.

So how long should you spend in Hippo Time?

Well, sorry to be vague, but it depends. When you start to reflect on the seven questions to develop Fruity Thinking, you are getting closer to moving on. However, the length of time you spend wallowing depends on several factors:

- The seriousness of the issue.
- The support you receive from others.
- The amount of pay-offs you are receiving for staying in the mud (attention, sympathy, supply of Victim T-shirts, etc.)
- Your willingness to explore how to move on.

I am not here to give you guidelines on how long you need to wallow (e.g. broken relationship – four weeks; scratched car – three days; missing out on promotion – one week). But remember this:

> *Hippo Time should never be a place of permanent residence.*
>
> *Wallowing is temporary; SUMO is forever.*

SUMO
wisdom

THE PERSONAL STUFF

My wife and I had a beautiful conservatory built on the back of our house. There was hassle with the builders during construction, but we were delighted when it was eventually finished – until it started to leak. The leaks were fixed and again we started to enjoy this new addition to our home. Three months later, I discovered another small leak in the roof, and I rang the company to ask them to repair it. There was no reply. The company had gone out of business. I finally tracked down another company prepared to tackle our problem roof, expecting a minor repair to cost a maximum of £100. To be then informed that the roof was, in fact, structurally unsafe and would cost several thousand pounds to rectify came as a nasty surprise. My wife and I were officially entering into Hippo Time. Did we tell lots of people? You bet. However, we quickly realized

> that every time we re-told what had happened,
> our anger increased. We stopped telling people
> and we felt better for it. Fortunately, our
> insurance covered the cost of a new roof.

In order to move on, there is more to be gained by you looking forward than there is from you looking back. You need to be honest with yourself and ask this question:

'What is it costing me in terms of energy and opportunity to remain stuck in Hippo Time?'

The answer to this question should help you decide on how long you spend wallowing.

Points to Ponder...

Think of an occasion when you were in Hippo Time. How long did you spend there? On reflection, could you have moved on sooner? If so, what stopped you?

How do you help someone during Hippo Time?

It is probably helpful to start with what *not* to do.

- Don't fake-listen (i.e. pretend you are listening, when in fact you are wondering what to have for tea tonight, or whether your kids remembered to take their PE kit to school). The person talking will eventually realize you are not listening when they notice your eyes. They will be glazed over. You'll be having an OBE – an 'Out of Body Experience'. You know what I mean: the wheel's turning but the hamster's dead.

- Don't keep interrupting the other person with phrases such as, 'The same thing happened to me', or, 'I know how you feel'. (How can you know how I feel? Is your conservatory structurally unsafe too?)

- Don't invade their Hippo Time and have yours instead. This is usually pre-empted with the comment, 'Well, you think that's bad – you should hear what happened to me today'. Your turn will come, just be patient.

- Don't keep using the phrase, 'That's awful' or 'That's terrible'. (Express some concern, but don't overdo it. What are you trying to do? Make them feel worse than they already are?)

My wife Helen confesses there are perhaps cheaper and healthier ways to spend your time wallowing, but retail therapy and eating chocolate remain the most popular amongst her group of friends.

THE PERSONAL STUFF

Here's what to do instead

- Work hard (and it can be hard work) to give the other person your full attention. If it's not a convenient time for you to listen, let them know when would be a good time.
- Allow the person to vent, i.e. get things off their chest.
- Allow the person to cry (if they need to) – no matter how uncomfortable it makes you feel.
- Use phrases such as, 'It's OK to be angry' or 'You seem very hurt by that'. (Use language you are comfortable with. I'm not suggesting you need to sound like a therapist.)
- Give the other person space. Some people (particularly men) prefer to spend Hippo Time on their own. It would be helpful to say, 'Look, I appreciate you're upset. You know where I am if you need me', and then allow them time to themselves.
- When you feel it is appropriate, you might then use humour to diffuse the situation or put things into perspective. (Remember you need to be really careful about this, so if in doubt, avoid doing it.)

Points to Ponder...

Think of who you could help when they're in Hippo Time. Remember that you could hinder the experience depending on your response to them. Of the advice given on how to help people, which do you need to be most aware of?

THE PERSONAL STUFF

I, personally, like to go for a walk on my own when I'm wallowing. Although I admit a 112-mile walk was a bit extreme when Bradford City were relegated, but then I did have a lot of things to work through.

In a nutshell

Hippo Time is a valid place to be for some people before they can *Shut Up, Move On*. To deny and suppress our hurt and disappointment is unhealthy. However, spending too long in Hippo Time, especially with the wrong people, will not aid our recovery.

- Before you can SUMO you may need to take a detour to Hippo Time.
- Remember: the more times you replay your story, the more you re-live it. Sometimes, we need to SUMO rather than re-tell.
- Sharing your Hippo Time with anyone and everyone is not appropriate; be choosy who you include in your Hippo Time. Shut Up telling everyone your issues and Move On to people who will be more supportive.
- Be aware that the longer you spend in Hippo Time, the harder it is to Move On.
- Hippo Time is temporary. SUMO lasts a lifetime.
- When helping people in Hippo Time, Shut Up the fake listening, the interrupting and the 'awfulising' and Move On to giving your full attention. Allow people time to vent, and be sensitive to the fact that they may prefer to be left alone.

SUMO SUMMARY

Chapter 5
Remember The Beachball

The first three SUMO principles have focused on increasing our personal self-awareness. They could be put under the heading 'Understanding Yourself'. This fourth SUMO success principle moves us on from our own inner world and helps us to explore the world of others. In my experience, your ability to achieve better results in life comes through helping other people to do the same. Whether your needs are emotional, psychological or practical, the chances of them being fulfilled increase when you help others meet their needs.

So how can we achieve this?

In order for this to happen we need to develop a greater understanding and awareness of the people we deal with in our day-to-day lives. We need to get inside the heads of the people we meet in order to see the world from their viewpoints. To explain this further, let me share with you a simple, memorable and powerful illustration.

What is the beachball?

Imagine you are in a large room packed with over a hundred people. In the centre of the room is a large, multi-coloured

Red, white and blue   Orange, green and yellow

beachball. When I say large, I mean huge. So big, in fact, that it stands at over thirty feet tall and touches the ceiling. Because of its size, the people are squeezed back to the edges of the room. Now here is the interesting part. When you ask people from one side of the room the colour of the beachball they reply, 'Red, white and blue'; yet the people on the opposite side of the room claim to see three different colours: 'Orange, green and yellow'. Despite looking at the same beachball, the perspective they are looking from influences the colours they see.

Most people will *not* say, 'Well, from my perspective the beachball is red, white and blue, but I realize it might be different from yours'. No. People tend to believe that what they see is reality.

Thanks to the influence of the Greek philosophers Aristotle, Socrates and Plato, our education system in the West has conditioned us to think in logical, either/or, concrete terms. Things are either right or wrong. If, from where you are standing, the beachball is orange, green and yellow, it cannot also be red, white and blue. To continue the colour theme further, we have a tendency to think in black or white and in right or wrong terms. It seems safe. You see, when we don't, we can be labelled indecisive. Being open to alternative viewpoints may be seen as a sign of weakness on our part.

People generally are not comfortable with 'grey areas'. These are places of uncertainty. It is not how we have been taught to see the world. Winning an argument by proving the other person wrong is seen as a virtue. Education is a place where we ask, 'Did you get the answers right?' as opposed to, 'What did you learn?' Such a system of thinking is helpful in some areas such as mathematics, physics or engineering. Whatever side of the beachball you are on, the answer to 3 + 3 is 6. However, when it comes to understanding people and how they see the world, we need to adopt a more flexible way of thinking.

You may be familiar with the phrase 'there are always two sides to a story'. Actually, there may be more. And each one may be valid.

The question is: what influences people's perspectives? You're about to find out.

What influences how we and others see the beachball?

There are numerous factors that influence our perspectives. These include our age, values, personality, gender, background, culture, beliefs and many more. For the purpose of this section, let's explore four of them.

Our age influences how we see the beachball

I grew up in the 1960s. When I was young the term 'a big mac' meant a large overcoat you wore when it was raining. My children still look rather bemused when they ask for a 'Big Mac' and I reply, 'Why, is it raining?'

The phrase 'going all the way' when I was growing up, meant staying on the bus until it got to the terminus. I understand it has different connotations these days. And I can still remember black and white television, having a choice of only three channels and actually having to physically move off my chair if I wanted to change station. (Boy, we had it tough in those days, but at least we kept fit.)

Age also influences our perspective on life. The introduction of new technology into the workplace may be viewed very differently by someone who has been using computers since they were a toddler, compared with the individual who never even used a calculator at school. I am not suggesting people of a certain age group cannot adapt to technology, but for some people, it has been much more a part of their lives than for others.

A job for life would have been the expectancy for many people prior to the 1980s. Now I meet people in their late 20s who nonchalantly talk about being made redundant for the second time in their career. And if you have teenagers in your household, think of their challenges as they come to terms with hormonal changes, discovering their sexuality and being caught somewhere between childhood and adulthood.

With age comes experience and invariably, the older you are, the more experience you have. How you see and respond to a situation could be very different from the person who, because of their age, has not had an opportunity to acquire the same amount of experience.

Points to Ponder...

How does your age influence your views, attitudes and perspectives on life? Think about the ages of those with whom you have close relationships. Might this be one reason why you have different perspectives on life?

SUMO wisdom

If you want to win friends and influence people, start by first trying to understand them.

Our values influence how we see the beachball

Let me explain this from a personal perspective.

My friend Eddie loves his car. It's a Porsche. Not a new one, but one he completely adores and treats almost as though it were his child. Cars do not hold the same appeal for me. I drive a Mazda. It's comfortable, has a few nice gadgets and gets me from A to B. If I find a scratch on my car I am not exactly delighted, but I will soon get over it. Depending on the size of the scratch, on a scale of 1–10 it will probably do well to register a 2. Now if that happened to Eddie's car, you would be well advised to keep out of his company and not invade his period of mourning – for about four months. What Eddie and I value is different, and that influences how we see the beachball.

I like gardening. If one of my lupins becomes infested by greenfly, I set about the task of eliminating those vile creatures with military precision. They are the enemy. They must be destroyed. Eddie would not bother.

We can assume that everyone shares the same values as us. The reality is they probably don't. We live and interact with people who may share some of our values but rarely all of them. My work colleague Kate believes if you are not five minutes early for a meeting then you are

THE PERSONAL STUFF

late. Other people tend to have a more laid back approach to timekeeping, much to Kate's annoyance. One person's reaction to someone being late could be 'so what's the big deal?' Kate may choose to respond a little more assertively.

Our values give us what we believe to be 'the right way' to see the world. It naturally follows, in that case, that people who see things differently from us must have a 'wrong view'. It is this mindset that thinks 'my way is right and yours is wrong' that hinders our ability to develop successful relationships. It also explains why people with similar values may be very different in terms of personality yet develop successful, long-term, meaningful relationships with each other.

SUMO wisdom *Never assume that other people value the same things as you. If you want to develop better relationships, find out what is important to the other person.*

Points to Ponder... *Think of a situation where you don't see eye-to-eye with another person. Is this due to a clash of values? Are you prepared to make any compromises? Are they? If not, you may simply have to accept the limitations of your relationship.*

Our personality influences how we see the beachball

Again, let me share with you a personal perspective.

I have two children. One is loud, outgoing and generally likes to be the centre of attention (she takes after her mother); whilst the other quietly goes about his business, prefers staying in the background and is quite comfortable with silence. Two very different personalities, with neither being right or wrong. These differences, however, mean they do not see and respond to situations in the same way. When they were younger, a journey in the car for one of them was an opportunity to sing and tell stories, whilst for the other it was a chance to be still and reflect on the scenery.

Can you relate to any of this?

THE PERSONAL STUFF

There are many models for understanding different personality types, the most popular one being devised by Carl Jung, the Swiss psychologist (1875–1961). His aim was to help people understand themselves and others more fully, and explain why people perceive and respond to the world differently. Let me give a simple overview of one way of thinking about the four personality types. Remember, no one fits solely into one type; we are a blend of all four. However, like a cake recipe, some 'flavours' are more noticeable than others. Let me also stress, this is not intended to be an in-depth look at your personality. I include it purely as some food for thought.

The Cheerleader

An extrovert who gains energy from being around others. They have a tendency to 'wear their emotions on their sleeve'. Cheerleaders thrive on praise and recognition. They can also be impulsive and spontaneous in their opinions and actions, i.e. they often act without thinking and jump quickly to conclusions. Cheerleaders tend not to be the most naturally organized and structured of people, and often attempt a number of tasks at once, starting a new one before finishing the previous one.

Main driver for a cheerleader   Get noticed, get appreciated.

Likely to say   'Well, if you are looking for someone to interview for the company magazine, look no further.'

Unlikely to say   'I've started so I'll finish', or 'Here's a detailed report I prepared earlier'.

How cheerleaders see the beachball   They often see the positive side of the situation and may fail to consider a more cautious perspective. However, their viewpoint may fluctuate depending on how they are feeling emotionally. Catch them in a low mood and it can seem like the world is about to end.

The Carer

Generally a sociable person who values people contact, although less extrovert than a Cheerleader. They prefer to be in the background as opposed to the centre of attention, and are comfortable listening to others as opposed to talking. On less important issues, they will allow others to take the initiative. (Observing two Carers deciding where to go for lunch is a fascinating exercise.)

They are likely to have a more easy-going approach to life than some people and will do their best to avoid conflict and confrontation. Carers may struggle to say 'no' to people's requests, preferring to say 'yes' rather than run the risk of causing offence. They tend to be more of a follower than a leader.

Main driver for a carer   Get along with others.

Likely to say   'Right, before we start the meeting; how was your weekend?'

Unlikely to say   'OK everyone, I'm in charge here. Now listen up, I have a plan.'

How carers see the beachball   Their perspective is influenced by how the situation affects their relationships. How they feel about an issue can be more important than the facts themselves.

The Commander

An extrovert like the Cheerleader, but who is more focused on 'getting things done' with less concern for people. They typically adore 'to-do lists' and love the feeling of achievement when they are able to cross things off their list. Commanders thrive on challenges but their lack of patience comes to the fore when progress is delayed. They tend to be decisive, goal-orientated people who prefer talking to listening. Commanders are likely to make tough demands of themselves and of others, and they enjoy taking charge of a situation.

Main driver for a commander   Get things done.

Likely to say   'Well, that's another two hours wasted. Just exactly how long does it take to give birth these days?'

Unlikely to say   'I would be really interested to hear what other people think.'

How commanders see the beachball   Could see exploring other people's perspectives as a waste of time, as it delays the need to take action. Focus on ideas that achieve 'quick wins'.

The Thinker

More of an introvert who gains their energy through reflection and having time to themselves, as opposed to being around people. Like the Carer they prefer to listen rather than talk and are more comfortable analysing data than dealing with people. Thinkers are more likely to take a deliberate, structured analytical approach to a task and are less distracted by feelings and emotions when assessing a situation.

They tend to be cautious in nature and often require copious amounts of detail before making a decision. Thinkers also enjoy giving comprehensive, detailed answers to questions of a technical nature – whether the other person requires it or not. Planning and organizational skills come naturally to a thinker. Being the centre of attention does not.

Main driver for a thinker   Get this task right.

Likely to say   'Can you let me think about that and I'll have a detailed report with you inside the next three months.'

Unlikely to say   'I've just had a crazy idea. How about we organize a staff Christmas pantomime and I can be the lead role?'

How thinkers see the beachball   May have a tendency to see problems rather than possibilities, and focus on what could go wrong as opposed to why it might work. Could spend so long analysing the beachball that they fail to make any decision.

OK, review the four personality types. No one is exclusively one type and there will be elements of all four that you can relate to. However, if someone was to push you into a corner and force you to decide which two you identify with most, which would they be? You might not always behave that way, but which style are you most comfortable with?

(If you want to complete a quick and easy exercise to help shed some light on your preferred personality style, visit www .theSUMOguy.com/personality-test.aspx.)

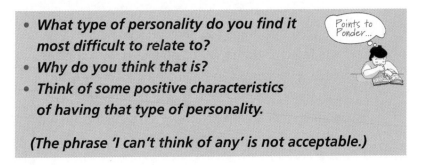

- **What type of personality do you find it most difficult to relate to?**
- **Why do you think that is?**
- **Think of some positive characteristics of having that type of personality.**

(The phrase 'I can't think of any' is not acceptable.)

> • **Think of a relationship that matters to you and consider how your different personality types might help or hinder the way you approach life and tackle problems.**

THE PERSONAL STUFF

I guess the personality types I relate to most are the Commander and the Cheerleader. My wife Helen is more of a Carer and Thinker. This provides quite a balance when it comes to making decisions, but it can also be a source of frustration for both of us. Whether it is to do with personality or gender I am not sure, but I am always amazed by Helen's behaviour on the telephone. No matter how much of a rush we are in, she insists on asking people how they and their family are before getting to the main purpose of her call. Meanwhile I am thrusting my watch in her face and reminding her that she has already spoken to this person twice today. However, her cautious approach and unwillingness to rush into a decision has saved us money.

Being the spontaneous 'get it done' person that I am, I was quite happy to go along with the first quote we received to have a new kitchen fitted. I liked the guy who came round to measure up and was impressed with his designs. As the quote was within our budget and he could start straight

> away I was happy to make a decision for the work
> to commence. My wife insisted that we get three
> more quotes. To me this was an unnecessary delay
> and a complete waste of time. We went with the
> final quote. It was better value (i.e. cheaper) and
> a more innovative design. My 'Thinker wife' had
> just saved us £500. It was an invaluable lesson for
> me and a reminder that how I see and respond to
> an event is not always the best way.

Our current state of mind influences how we see the beachball

Imagine you have just gained a promotion at work. You are delighted. You feel good about yourself. Then, on the way home you are involved in a minor car accident. The damage is minimal and no one is hurt. You view the incident as a minor inconvenience and nothing more. But what if you hadn't got the promotion? What if you had just been dumped by your partner? How would you respond to the minor accident now? Or if you are stuck in faulty thinking and your Inner Critic is bellowing in your ear, how receptive are you to the 'constructive criticism' your boss wants to give you?

Perhaps you are in 'Hippo Time' and you receive some unwelcome news. How will you respond now? Or maybe you have just got back from the slimming club and won Slimmer of the Week for losing the most weight. When you return home, one of your children asks to borrow the car. What is your likely answer? Would it be the same answer if you had put on weight?

Our view of situations can fluctuate greatly depending on how we are feeling at that particular time. Remember that when you're next communicating to someone, or listening to their story.

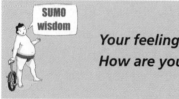

SUMO wisdom

Your feelings influence your perceptions. How are you feeling today?

Points to Ponder...

If you decide to tackle an issue with someone, consider how they might be currently feeling. And what about your current emotional state? Are you in the best frame of mind to tackle this? Choose your time carefully.

THE PERSONAL STUFF

This next example illustrates the consequences of not seeing someone else's perspective and also why it is necessary to let people know how you see things.

I had bought two tickets to see a football international to be played at Anfield, the home of Liverpool FC. There was only one problem. The game clashed with Helen's birthday and I knew she wasn't a keen fan of football. Having expressed sympathy for such an unfortunate coincidence, I then promptly invited my next-door neighbour to join me at the game. Helen, although disappointed, seemed to appreciate this was a one-off occurrence and took a night in with the children, on her birthday, in her stride. When I was at the match I suddenly had a thought, 'I wonder if Helen would have liked to have been here?' I quickly dismissed such a notion and reasoned with myself, 'If she had wanted to come she would surely have asked'. Meanwhile, back at home Helen, I learned later, was thinking the following, 'I wouldn't have minded going to the game tonight. But Paul would have invited me if he wanted me to come.' It was a cracking match. When I returned the kids were in bed and Helen was doing the ironing. Only then did we each share our own perspective on the night's events. Our conversation went something like this:

> **Paul** *'But if I'd known you wanted to come, of course I would have invited you.'*
> **Helen** *'Then why didn't you ask me?'*
> **Paul** *'Well, you don't like football.'*
> **Helen** *'So?'*
> **Paul** *'Well, I thought you would have said something if you were that keen to go.'*
> **Helen** *'I shouldn't have to. You should know.'*
> **Paul** *'Know what exactly?'*
> **Helen** *'That it would have been nice to be asked.'*

> **Paul** *'Look, I'm really sorry. Can we have an early night and forget all about it?'*
> **Helen** *'No.'*
>
> We both assumed that the other person understood our view of the beachball. I believed if Helen wanted to go to the game she would have asked me, and Helen believed if I wanted her to go, I would have invited her. We now recognize that not only do we need to take time out to see the other person's perspective, we also need to take responsibility to communicate how we are seeing things.

How to recognize when you're only seeing your side of the beachball

It is easy to spot when this is occurring. Simply notice the language you start to use. Take a look at the list of phrases and tick when it's one you've said or thought in the last few months.

- 'Why can't you see it my way?' (Have you tried to see it 'their way'?) ☐
- 'I don't understand my kids. They never listen to a word I say.' (How can you understand someone when you are doing all the talking?) ☐
- 'Why can't you be reasonable?' (Presumably you have decided what 'reasonable' means, i.e. to see and respond to the world the way you do.) ☐

- 'What planet are you on?' (Well, maybe it is time to enter their space and find out.) ☐
- 'That music is awful. You've no taste.' (In truth we all have taste, it's just that not everyone shares yours.) ☐
- 'They can be so boring.' (You mean, they don't meet your criteria of what interesting and exciting is like.) ☐
- 'There is only one way to handle this problem.' (In fact, there could be a number of alternatives, but you are going with the first one that comes to mind.) ☐

Get the picture? Actually, we probably don't get the full picture unless we are prepared to remove our blinkers. Most of us (including myself) need reminding of how many different ways the world can be viewed and the factors that influence people's perspective. But does appreciating others' viewpoints mean I have to agree with them?

Understanding does not mean agreeing

Discovering someone's perspective, and understanding the reasons for their views, does not necessarily mean we agree and embrace them ourselves. You will meet some very sincere people who hold very strong opinions on life. You may believe them to be sincerely wrong. However, if you want to persuade them at least to consider another viewpoint, but begin with the attitude, 'I am right, you are wrong', it will do little to encourage meaningful dialogue.

When you begin with the attitude, 'Let me first try to understand why you think and behave the way you do', you're more likely to encourage an open and honest discussion. When you feel people have listened to you and tried to understand you, then you are more likely to listen to them.

SUMO wisdom *People are less defensive when you seek to understand their viewpoint rather than try to dismantle it.*

Having looked at *why* people see the beachball differently, let's look at *how* we go about understanding another person's viewpoint.

How to move forward

If you have not done so already, identify a relationship that you know needs to improve. Perhaps you have failed to see the other person's side of the beachball up until now, or you have failed to communicate how things look from your perspective. A willingness to Shut Up the old approach and Move On to a different strategy may now be required. Here are some practical ideas on how to help the process. The relevance of some of the ideas will depend on the context of the conversation.

• Firstly, do not attempt to have a conversation when both of you are angry. You will both be in primitive brain and 'discussion' is likely to become an argument. At least one of you needs to be in 'rational brain'.

• Work hard at actively listening and indicate to the other person through your body language that you are. Make some eye contact, avoid distractions (such as the computer or the television being on) and give this person your full attention. Their perception of whether or not you are listening is crucial.

- Don't interrupt the other person and take over the conversation. Allow them to vent.
- Don't finish off the other person's sentences. This can give the impression you are rushing them and sometimes you get it wrong.
- Work hard at trying to understand their perspective. Put aside preconceived ideas of what you think their view is.
- As you listen, look for what you can agree with, rather than focus on what divides you.
- When they have finished speaking, the first question to ask is, 'Is there anything else you would like to add?' This prevents you from jumping in immediately with your perspective. It also provides the other person with an opportunity to summarize their points, and perhaps re-emphasize an issue that is important to them.
- Before moving on to share your perspective, ask questions to gain clarification, e.g. 'When you said... can you explain that a little more?' or 'Can you give me an example of that, please?' This is not done to make the other person defensive, but in order genuinely to understand their view.
- It is now your turn to share how you see things. Ensure the behaviour you have modelled is followed by the other person. (This might require you having to be assertive if they start to interrupt you or do not allow you to finish.)

Helpful phrases to use

The following phrases may prove helpful in your conversation. However, use language and terminology you are comfortable with. These are just some examples:

'Help me understand your perspective on this.'

'Can we explore some options on how best to deal with this situation?'

'I would be really interested to know what you think.'

'I'm conscious I'm only seeing things from my perspective; what would your view be?'

'Maybe I've been a bit inflexible in my approach up until now.'

And when you need to communicate your perspective...

'Can I shed some light on how I see things?'

'Let me fill you in on how things look from my perspective.'

'I'd value you giving me some time to share my take on things.'

'I appreciate you might not be aware of all the facts from my viewpoint, so let me elaborate.'

These ideas and phrases are intended to help the process. They will not guarantee a successful outcome, but they do increase the chances.

Sometimes it is completely acceptable and appropriate to stand your ground. But not always. How are your stubbornness and unwillingness to be flexible helping the situation? How is insisting that you are right helping to move things forward? Which phrases might you consider using? Is the other person aware of your perspective?

Points to Ponder...

Angela, a friend of mine, has not spoken to her mother for two years.

The reason for this silence is all to do with her mother – or so Angela believes. Angela believes she is in the right and her mother is in the wrong; therefore, why should she have to make the first move towards some kind of reconciliation with her mum? Angela has two small children. They do not know their grandma.

THE PERSONAL STUFF

Move things forward by challenging the golden rule

You may have come across a concept called 'the golden rule'. Many people believe it to be the best advice you can have on how to build successful relationships. Personally I'm not so sure. Here's why.

The golden rule states the following:

'Treat people as you would want to be treated.'

This seems a fairly noble view, and it's true regarding the ethics and morality of our behaviour. However, in terms of communication style and personality preferences, it's not always helpful. Does an introverted, middle-aged 'Thinker' who has recently got married and moved to the countryside want to be treated in the same way as a young, recently divorced 'Cheerleader' who has just started work in the city?

The SUMO rule is this:

'Not everyone wants to be treated in the same way as you do.

Treat people as they want to be treated.'

Most people do want to be dealt with fairly, honestly and with respect. But after that, it is up to us to find out what works best for them. When you do, you are better equipped to achieve a more favourable outcome. So challenge conventional wisdom and be prepared to bring a new perspective to things.

Consider a relationship where a beachball conversation would be helpful and reflect on the following questions:

1 Reflect for a moment on what factors are influencing this person's view of the beachball. How old is this person? Could that be influencing how they're seeing the world? What do you believe is important to them, and what do they value?

Consider the four personality types: Cheerleader, Carer, Commander, Thinker. Which combination would they be?

How would you say this person is feeling at the moment? Are they in Hippo Time? Perhaps they're struggling with faulty thinking? Maybe they're feeling great. In one sentence describe their current state of mind.

2 In what ways have you tried to understand their perspective and see their side of the beachball?

3 Have you clearly communicated your perspective? (Remember, using the phrase 'I shouldn't have to, they should know' is you failing to take responsibility. It could be argued you are playing the role of Victim with such an approach.)

4 If there was one single action you could take to help influence and improve the relationship what would it be? (Your response to the event can influence the outcome.)

The joy of a new perspective

Life can become quite interesting when you look at things from a new angle. I came across this piece recently. I hope you enjoy it. It is entitled 'The George Carlin Theory'.*

The most unfair thing about life is the way it ends...

---

*The American comedian George Carlin did not write this piece and the actual author remains unknown.

I mean, life is tough. It takes up a lot of your time and what do you get at the end of it? Death. I mean, what's that, a bonus? I think the life cycle is all backwards. You should die first, get it out of the way. Then you move to an old people's home. You get kicked out when you're too young, you get a gold watch and then you go to work. You work for forty years until you're young enough to enjoy your retirement. You have fun, party plenty, then you get ready for senior school. Then you go to junior school, you become a kid, you play and you have no responsibilities. You become a little baby, you go back into the womb, spend your last nine months floating... and you finish off as an orgasm.

In a nutshell

The ability to succeed in life is inextricably linked to our ability to deal with people. To know how best to deal with others we need to start with trying to understand them. When we appreciate how and why people view the world differently and respond appropriately to that, we are able to connect and engage with them at a completely new level.

- A brilliant life comes through better relationships.
- In order to meet your needs, help others to achieve theirs.
- Two opposing views do not necessarily mean one has to be wrong.
- Remember the beachball. *Shut Up* believing your perspective is the only one and *Move On* to seeing how the world looks through someone else's eyes.
- Four factors that influence how we see things are:
  - Our age.
  - Our values.
  - Our personality (don't forget to do the test, visit www.theSUMOguy.com).
  - Our current state of mind.
- Understanding someone's viewpoint does not necessarily mean you agree with it.
- When people feel you are trying to understand them, they are more likely to try and understand you.
- *Shut Up* waiting for the other person to take the initiative. *Move On* to being a peacemaker.

SUMO SUMMARY

Chapter 6
Learn Latin

We have now explored four SUMO principles. But here is the harsh reality. Despite the insights and ideas you have gained so far, they may result in little or no change in your life. This fifth principle will explore why we can be full of good intentions and yet fail to make those intentions reality. You will discover the reasons why we procrastinate and how to overcome them. Or, to put it another way, how you can *Shut Up* the excuses and *Move On* to action.

Let me begin by sharing a personal experience of my struggle to take action.

THE PERSONAL STUFF

In the spring of 1991 I set up my own business, working as a freelance trainer and speaker. Times were tough. The economic boom of the 80s was over and Britain was officially in recession. My 'office' doubled as a bedroom, so I had a desk, a telephone and a double bed. It was a challenge (particularly for Bob and Linda in the double bed). As I sat at my desk, I faced a list of names and telephone numbers of people who I needed to contact. Deep down – actually, not even deep down – I dreaded having to make a single call. I began to fantasize (not all fantasies are positive you know) about the reactions I would receive. 'They're tied up at the moment'; 'Can you call back... in four years'; or just a simple, 'No thank you'.

I hated cold calling and quite quickly became enveloped by the 'phantom of procrastination'. As it was 1.30 p.m., I convinced myself that most people would still be on lunch and to wait another half-hour. Two o'clock arrived and I then persuaded myself that I was overcome with an incredible urge for coffee. Making my way downstairs to the kitchen, I became distracted by plants that needed watering and plates that needed washing. Thirty minutes passed. It was 2.30 p.m. and all excuses had dried up (or so I thought). It was actually time to make those cold calls.

But then came a flash of inspiration. A conversation unfolded within my mind. How many people are still at work at 2.30 p.m. on a Friday afternoon? Even those that are, are not likely to want to discuss their training requirements. Their thoughts will already be focused on the weekend. I will leave those calls until Monday, I reasoned to myself. Phew, what a relief; the difficult and uncomfortable task of cold calling had been put off for a few days.

I had convinced myself that there was no point in taking any immediate action and in doing so, had missed out on the opportunity of winning more business. However, I had achieved my goal – to avoid rejection and not do anything uncomfortable. Sound familiar?

Procrastination came easily to me, but then I saw the film *Dead Poets Society*. It was to provide the perfect antidote. At one stage in the film the late Robin Williams, who plays the lead role of an English teacher at an American all boys public school, teaches his pupils a Latin phrase. In an attempt to inspire these young men not to take their lives for granted, he teaches them the phrase *carpe diem*. Loosely translated, this means 'seize the day'. I was inspired by the film and made a poster with the phrase '*Carpe Diem*, Seize the Day' written on it, which I hung on my office wall. (Bob and Linda were cool about it.)

The next day I was watching the BBC Television comedy *Only Fools and Horses*. Two brothers run a market stall in south-east London; however, times are tough and money is short. In an attempt to motivate his younger brother Rodney, Delboy utters a version of the SAS motto 'Who Dares Wins'. Delboy's exact words were 'He who dares, wins'. I liked the phrase. It was what I needed to hear. I made my second makeshift poster for my office wall and when I heard the 'phantom of procrastination' whisper in my ear, I now felt I at least had two phrases to inspire me into taking action.

What are some of the things you try to put off doing? Do you procrastinate more at home or at work? How often does it happen?

Points to Ponder...

So why do we procrastinate?

Let's explore six reasons why people 'put things off' and fail to *carpe diem* and take action in their lives. (These reasons have been inspired by my friends at The Mind Gym, www.themindgym.com.)

Reason 1 – Avoiding discomfort

Achieving success means that, at times, we have to leave our 'comfort zone'. We may have to move out of our world of familiarity, safety and security and do things that we would not normally do. When we do something new or different, it can feel strange. This can result in a negative response initially because many people subconsciously live by the mantra:

'If it feels good, do it.'

Likewise, they can also live by the reverse of this mantra:

'If it doesn't feel good, don't do it.'

Although there are exceptions, our tendency as human beings is to take the path of least resistance. We look for the magic pill, the magic patch, the magic exercise machine. Products that promise 'successful outcomes' with little or no long-term effort on our part will always be popular.

Successful people think differently. They understand that if they are to achieve a positive result in any area of life, then they have to be prepared to face their 'discomfort' head on. Whether it is getting fit or going for a new job, life will present us with challenges. If we are to succeed, this will involve us taking action or thinking in a way that moves us beyond our normal zone of comfort and familiarity.

SUMO wisdom

Blessed are the people who do the uncomfortable, for they will often be successful.

Points to Ponder...

What are some of the things you feel uncomfortable having to do? What is the cause of your discomfort? Now reflect on this question: Where do life's opportunities really lie? Inside or outside your comfort zone?

Reason 2 – Emotional barriers

Whether we decide to take action or not can be dependent on how we feel. For example, I am going to write that report, tidy the garage or go on that diet *when I feel motivated*. Or I am waiting to *feel creative* before I tackle that problem. Put simply, emotions can take our actions hostage.

> **SUMO wisdom**
>
> ***When you remain a prisoner to your emotions, you may never know the freedom of success.***

> **Points to Ponder...**
>
> ***Can you relate to 'emotional barriers?' What have you failed to tackle in your life because you haven't felt like doing it?***

Reason 3 – Fear of failure

It is easy to develop the following mindset: 'if I don't attempt something, then I can never be accused of failing'. That is true. Equally, however, if I never attempt anything, I will never experience the feelings of achievement and success. Some people are quite happy to stand on the sidelines and point out where others go wrong, yet they themselves lack the courage to dare to fail.

> **SUMO wisdom**
>
> ***If you want to achieve anything in life, remember: setbacks come with the territory.***

From our childhood, we can become conditioned (there's that word again – remember Pavlov's dog?) to believe that if we attempt something and fail, that this is in some way wrong. Education has, in some cases, encouraged us to find '*the* right answer' rather than to experiment and discover many right answers. (We explored some of this in Chapter 5.)

Behind some people's behaviour is the underlying belief that 'I must be right, I must be perfect'. Attempting something that may expose weaknesses or lack of knowledge will be avoided by some people. Fear of failure, or perhaps more importantly, the fear of *being seen by others to have failed*, will trap some people into never taking action.

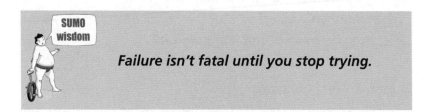

SUMO wisdom

Failure isn't fatal until you stop trying.

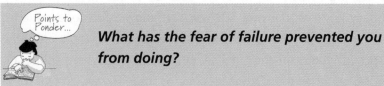

Points to Ponder...

What has the fear of failure prevented you from doing?

Reason 4 – Complacency

'There's no rush', 'I'll wait till the kids have left home', 'I'll quit smoking in the New Year'. There always seems to be some reason why we can put off taking action today. What can drive this attitude is a false belief that there is plenty of time to accomplish all we want to achieve. But when tomorrow does come, we find another excuse to avoid taking action.

Complacency can also occur due to the mistaken belief that life is something that happens to you as opposed to something you can influence. (We will look at this in more detail in our final SUMO principle.)

A lack of goals and sense of purpose in our lives results in people drifting along in a haze of complacency. Returning to our foundation formula, to the SUMO principles $E + R = O$, well if life is the Event and complacency is your Response, how satisfied are you likely to be with the Outcome?

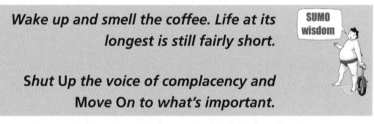

Wake up and smell the coffee. Life at its longest is still fairly short.

Shut Up *the voice of complacency and* **Move On** *to what's important.*

SUMO wisdom

In what areas of your life have you allowed complacency to creep in? Your career? Relationships? Home improvements? Finance? Fitness? All of them?

Points to Ponder...

Reason 5 – Action illusion

Some people can always appear busy. The question is, busy doing what? Rather than admit that they don't want to do a task, they use a lack of time as their excuse. People can talk about what they are going to do, hold meetings to discuss how they are going to do it and even draw up plans outlining what they will do. This may all be very useful initially, but there comes a time when we need to start taking action.

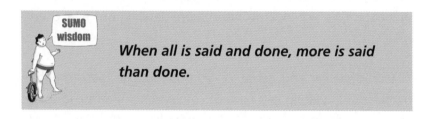

SUMO wisdom

When all is said and done, more is said than done.

We saw from our first SUMO principle that, on a day-to-day basis, we do so much on auto-pilot, i.e. without thinking. Maybe we need to ask ourselves, 'Am I confusing activity with effectiveness?'

Reason 6 – Fuzzy focus

This occurs when we've got so many things competing for our attention that we're not sure what to focus on. There's so much you could do but without prioritizing your goals you become unfocused and this lack of clarity can cause indecision and inactivity.

Points to Ponder...

Are your activities and your busyness hiding the fact that you do not want to address the really important issues in your life right now?

So we have explored why people procrastinate; now we need to examine how to overcome it.

Where do we go from here?

Some people may be tempted to say the following: 'Okay, big deal. I procrastinate. Doesn't everyone?' Well, actually – no! Some people have decided to take responsibility and to take action. Now, there is no 'Procrastinators Anonymous' support group (although there have been a number of people who have thought about setting one up, but never got round to it). So how are we going to tackle this unhelpful, debilitating habit that can rob us of achieving success and happiness in life? Here are some strategies that people use to defeat procrastination.

How to conquer the procrastination habit

Just start it

That's right, just do something. Do not worry about completing the task or how much time it will take to finish – just start it. Yes, I know you are not in the mood and you are not feeling motivated. Tough. SUMO! Momentum can bring motivation, and the sense of achievement from actually starting the activity can lead to you feeling better about yourself. This, in turn, can give you the drive and desire to finish what you've started.

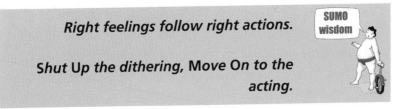

Right feelings follow right actions.

Shut Up the dithering, Move On to the acting.

SUMO wisdom

THE PERSONAL STUFF

For two years I had contemplated tidying my garage. Two years! Then one day, when I had a spare half-hour before lunch, I decided to make a start. (Even though I knew it would probably take at least half a day.) Within five minutes, I found a level of enthusiasm rising up within me I had not known before. I discovered things I never realized we even had... an old motorbike, a garden gnome, two children. (Alright, the garden gnome is perhaps an exaggeration.)

Picture what success looks like and how it feels

Think about the task you know you need to tackle. Perhaps it is quitting smoking, losing weight, speaking in public or flying for the first time. Now I want you to close your eyes and imagine what success will look and feel like. What do you see? What are you able to do now that you were unable to do before? How does it feel to have conquered that fear of flying or speaking? When you've quit smoking, how will you feel about yourself? Whatever your challenge, imagine the outcome you want rather than the activities required to get you there. Focusing on your destination rather than the journey can inspire you to take action.

Now imagine your life in five years' time if you decide to do nothing. What does your world look like now? What are the consequences of you not taking action? Visualize it. How does that make you feel? Is that what you want for your future?

Do the nasties first

Each day people are faced with tasks they would prefer not to do. It could be a telephone call to make or a person to meet. All of us can be tempted to tackle the more pleasurable tasks first and then leave the nasties until later. Guess what? Sometimes we find that we've not had enough time to tackle our nasties. What a pity. Never mind, you'll get round to it tomorrow. Then when you wake up the next day, what have you got to look forward to? Tackling the 'nasties'. So, what does that do to your levels of motivation?

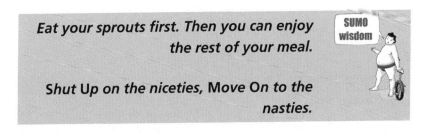

Eat your sprouts first. Then you can enjoy the rest of your meal.

Shut Up on the niceties, Move On to the nasties.

Not all 'nasties' are as bad as we would expect. But some are – that's why they are called 'nasties'. I am not asking you to convince yourself that 'nasties' are really nice. I am saying tackle them first – unless you can prove in a court of law that the more pleasurable task you embarked upon is, in fact, more important.

Reward your progress

Once you decide to take action, reward your progress. Just finished a nasty? Good, so what is your mini reward? (I suggest a mini reward or else this conquering procrastination routine could get rather expensive.)

It might be to go and see a film, have a coffee break or you might simply decide to ring that friend you wanted a chat with. I am going to reward myself with a teacake after I have finished writing this chapter. (Oh, the life of an international speaker and author.)

Remember, if it's a task that will take a long time to complete, then we need to set ourselves some milestones and reward our progress. Rewarding yourself only after you have finished the task may not be motivating enough. A friend of mine who wanted to lose weight bought herself a new music album for every 7lb shed. Another friend filled a jar with all the money saved from quitting smoking and spent it on a family holiday.

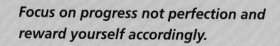

SUMO wisdom

Focus on progress not perfection and reward yourself accordingly.

Make a date with a mate

The sad fact of life is that only a small percentage of people reading this book will take any action as a result. But what if you knew that you were attending a workshop in four weeks' time and had to report to the group on what actions you had taken as a result of reading this book? The chances are, the percentage of people who would take action would increase significantly. (Hence, I often run follow-up sessions to my workshops.)

A 'mate' does not need to be a friend, but someone who you are happy to share your issue with and who is committed to following up on your progress. They must also have your permission to challenge you if you're not taking the action you said you would.

My work as a life coach brings positive results in people's lives, partly because they have someone to support them and someone they feel accountable to. Ultimately, my clients are only accountable to themselves, but the discipline of having to feed back their progress results in more focused actions being taken by them.

THE PERSONAL STUFF

SUMO wisdom

Shut Up trying to do it on your own, Move On to finding a mate to support you.

Challenge your complacency

Perhaps the most powerful way I can challenge your complacency is to ask you to consider the following.

Imagine seven people lined up in a row:

Now imagine each person represents a day of the week.

| Mon | Tue | Wed | Thu | Fri | Sat | Sun |

Now imagine each day of the week represents a decade of your life.

| 0–10 | 11–20 | 21–30 | 31–40 | 41–50 | 51–60 | 61–70 |

So which day of the week are you on? I am on very late Friday night. Within a matter of months I'll be on the Saturday of my life. For some of you it has already arrived. Cheery thought, eh?

Now, before all those who are reading this get too depressed because you are already at the weekend, consider this. If you are living a healthy lifestyle, you can add another two people to your line-up (making a total of nine people), as there is a good chance you will get a Bank Holiday Monday and Tuesday as well.

| 0–10 | 11–20 | 21–30 | 31–40 | 41–50 | 51–60 | 61–70 | 71–80 | 81–90 |

Remember, it's never too late to take action. I am inspired by people such as Winston Churchill. He became Prime Minister for a second time on the Bank Holiday Monday of his life.

So whatever day of the week you are on, perhaps it is time to take the necessary action to make sure the journey is not just a good one, but a great one.

You owe it to yourself and those around you to challenge your complacency. (Our next SUMO principle will help you to make the rest of your 'week' a significant and successful one.)

Zig Ziglar said, 'At the end of your days, do **SUMO wisdom** *not be the kind of person who says I wish I had, I wish I had. Be the kind of person who says I'm glad I did, I'm glad I did.'*

Those are some ideas on how to conquer our procrastination habit. Now it's time to use them. Work through the following questions, preferably with a 'mate'. Only when you have finished the exercise can you have a mini reward.

SUMO exercise

1 Choose a task or issue that you need to take action on.
2 Why is this important to you?
3 What are the consequences if you take no action?
4 Picture and feel what success will look like when you've achieved your objective.
5 Which 'procrastinators' hinder your progress? (i.e. avoiding discomfort, emotional barriers, fear of failure, action illusion and complacency.)
6 What actions will you take to tackle this issue? (What are your top three priorities?)
7 When will you start?
8 How will you reward your progress?
9 Who will be your 'mate'?

You can e-mail me with your progress and successes at: Paul.McGee@theSUMOguy.com.

THE PERSONAL STUFF

So how has learning and living by the Latin phrase *carpe diem* helped me? The turning point in my business came in 1994. I had just received an information pack from an organization that ran business seminars in America, Europe and Asia. They were now looking for British-based speakers to develop their work further in the UK. They particularly wanted to hear from trainers or speakers who were comfortable addressing large audiences (I mean in terms of numbers, not weight) and who enjoyed 'performing' and delivering their material in an entertaining way. With all due modesty, I have

to admit I thought the job specification had
been written specifically with me in mind. (My
next book will be on the subject of developing
personal humility.)

Then I came to the section marked 'method of
application'. It said the following: 'Please apply by
sending in a one-hour video of yourself, speaking
ideally in front of 50 to 100 people.' It then
added, 'If you do not possess such a video, you are
probably not ready to join us yet.' The excitement
that had been welling up inside of me immediately
drained away. At that point in my career, I spoke
mainly to groups of around a dozen people,
and I quickly realized that my two main clients
were unlikely to allow their training sessions to
be filmed. My hopes of international travel and
speaking in front of large audiences had been
crushed with the reading of one sentence.

Realizing there was no possible way I could meet
their application criteria, I reluctantly placed the
information pack in the bin. Then I looked up.
On the wall in front of me, were two makeshift
posters with the phrases 'Carpe Diem, Seize the
Day' and 'Who Dares Wins'. I couldn't ignore
them. They seemed to compel me to reach
back into the bin and pull out the discarded
information pack. The wording under the

'method of application' section had not changed – but the mindset of the person reading it had.

As I read the form now, I was determined that I would apply for the position. Rather than accept the reality of the situation, I was now beginning to think of possible solutions around it. The form still stated, *'please apply by sending a one-hour video of yourself, speaking ideally in front of 50 to 100 people'*. However, my eyes immediately focused on the word, *'ideally'*. 'Paul, we don't live in an ideal world,' I thought to myself, and a plan began to unfold in my mind. Hire a room, invite a few friends and get my wife, Helen, to film a one-hour session of me delivering my best material.

Yet almost immediately a barrage of 'what ifs' flooded into my mind. What if you cannot find a room to hire? What if your friends cannot make it? What if you fail? Reasons to procrastinate began to line up in my head. I realized that taking action would require me to move out of my comfort zone. There was also the possibility that I might have to explain my failure to a number of people if the organization rejected my application. But how would I feel if I did not apply? Would such an opportunity come along again, and if so, when? I then allowed myself to dwell on another 'what if' question. 'What if I succeed?'

My *carpe diem* mindset was now very much in charge and I began to put my plan into action. Hiring a room was straightforward, but what about renting a crowd? I rang all my friends and put forward my proposition. 'There will be free food, free drink, just laugh in the right places.' Having rung all my friends and convinced both to attend (you remember Bob and Linda, don't you?), I then realized that although 50 people was unrealistic, an audience of two was perhaps a little on the low side.

Eventually, with the support of some family and a few people who would subject themselves to anything at the thought of free food (I knew a couple of students), my audience swelled to a grand total of eight. After filming, I submitted my video (some, but not all, of my audience laughed in the right places), making it clear to the organization that what they were watching was a contrived scenario.

But what did I have to lose? Well, my Inner Critic kept reminding me that actually, I could 'look really stupid', but I chose to recall the phrase 'Who Dares Wins'. Several weeks later I finally received a telephone call. The organization had watched my video and wanted to meet me. Eventually they hired me. They became my largest client and working for them was a turning point, not just in my business, but in my life also. Within three years of sending the video filmed in front of eight people in Warrington, I was presenting seminars to hundreds of people in places like Hong Kong, Malaysia and Singapore. On this occasion I had conquered my procrastination habit and was now reaping the rewards. But I still look back on my life before this time and wish I had learnt the lesson sooner. How much longer will you wait?

SUMO wisdom

Don't leave your dreams in the bin. Shut Up the voice that says 'No way', Move On to the voice that says 'Why not?'

Points to Ponder...

It will have been easy to read through this chapter and ignore the exercises, and not really take time to consider the questions raised. If that's what you've done, I guarantee that reading this book will not help you succeed in life. But if you do take action, well, who knows what you might achieve? Our final SUMO principle will provide some answers to that question.

In a nutshell

Great ideas, great goals and great intentions are meaningless without great actions. People achieve success in life not just because they take charge of their thinking, but because their thinking propels them into taking action.

- Life rewards intelligent action, not intention.
- People fail to take action for a variety of reasons: avoiding discomfort, emotional barriers, fear of failure, complacency, action illusion and fuzzy focus.
- Procrastination is a debilitating habit that can rob you of success and happiness.
- Tactics to conquer the procrastination habit include;
  - *Just start it.* Shut *Up* the dithering, *Move On* to the acting.
  - *What does success look and feel like?*
  - *Do the nasties first.* Shut *Up* on the niceties, *Move On* to the nasties.
  - *Reward your progress.*
  - *Make a date with a mate.* Shut *Up* trying to do it on your own, *Move On* to finding a mate to support you.
  - *Challenge your complacency.* Shut *Up* the voice of complacency, *Move On* to what is important.
- Shut *Up* believing reading this book is enough; *Move On* to doing something.

SUMO SUMMARY

Chapter 7
Ditch Doris Day

OK, I confess, this may seem a strange title for our sixth SUMO principle. So let me explain.

Why Doris Day?

In 1956, Jay Livingston and Ray Evans wrote the song 'Que Sera Sera' for the Alfred Hitchcock movie *The Man Who Knew Too Much*. It was sung by Doris Day. One of the lines is as follows:

'Que sera, sera,

Whatever will be, will be,

The future's not ours to see...'

Doris Day, who at the time of writing is in her early 90s, is still esteemed as a wonderful actress and singer and is adored by fans around the world. Doris, this is not personal. But our final SUMO principle is this: if we want to experience a brilliant life we must rid ourselves of the *laissez faire* attitude, 'Whatever will be, will be'. Let's be honest. How inspiring is that? I recognize unexpected events will occur in your life and mine, but I believe we can still plan and work towards a future *we* want to see. This is what our final success principle is all about: creating our future.

Firstly, let's remind ourselves of the five previous SUMO success principles:

1 Take responsibility for your life (*Change Your T-shirt*).
2 Take charge of your thinking *(Develop Fruity Thinking)*.
3 Understand how setbacks affect you and how to recover from them. *(Hippo Time Is OK)*.
4 Increase your understanding and awareness of other people's world *(Remember The Beachball)*.
5 Change comes through action not intention *(Learn Latin)*.

Now your aim is to take those five principles and apply them in helping you to 'succeed in life'. But first you need to decide what kind of future you want.

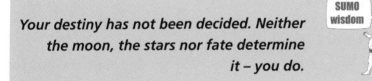

Your destiny has not been decided. Neither the moon, the stars nor fate determine it – you do.

SUMO wisdom

What kind of future do you want?

Several years ago, I heard the American sociologist and human rights campaigner Dr Anthony Campolo address a large gathering of sales people. He recalled some research he had come across in which a group of elderly people, all of whom were aged 95 or over, were asked the following question: 'If you were to live your life over again, what would you do differently next time?'

Now that is an interesting question. And it is one I would like you to think about. After all, why wait until you're too old to do anything about it before considering such an important issue?

Now you are probably wondering what these elderly people answered. (If you're not, you should be. Where is your sense of curiosity?) According to Campolo, the three top answers were summarized as follows:

Have fewer regrets

It seems this was related more to what people didn't do as opposed to what they did do in their lives.

Take time out to reflect more

Some people felt they just drifted along with the crowd and spent little, if any, time considering what *they* really wanted from life.

Leave a legacy

People wanted to feel that their life on Earth had counted for something and that in some way their life would be remembered after they had gone.

Now, how old are you? I want you to imagine what might be a scary scenario. Tomorrow will be your last day on this planet and you are asked the same question: 'If you were to live your life over again, what would you do differently next time?' What would your top three answers be? (You can write them below if you like.)

My top three answers would be:

1

2

3

I find it interesting that most people will write a will about what they want to happen to their affairs after they die. It requires some time and effort to sort out a will. However, fewer people seem to put the same effort and attention into what they want to happen whilst they are alive. Although they might not consciously think it, some people's behaviour indicates they are living by the philosophy 'Whatever will be, will be'.

How about you?

Food for thought? I hope so. Now your answers to the following questions will determine whether you 'Ditched Doris Day' long ago or whether you are still embracing a 'Que Sera, Sera' view of life.

As you answer the questions, remember this:

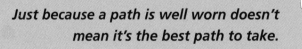

Just because a path is well worn doesn't mean it's the best path to take.

SUMO wisdom

1 Have you ever considered what success means to you? Yes/No
2 Do you have some specific, clearly defined goals that you wish to achieve in life? (The goal 'being happy' is not a specific goal.) Yes/No
3 If you have some goals, have you shared them with someone close to you? Yes/No
4 Do you have some plans in place to help you achieve your goals? Yes/No
5 Have you thought about the kind of memories you would like your family and friends to have of you? Yes/No

If you have more noes than yeses you have a decision to make: either do something about it or don't. The choice is yours. This is your life.

My goal is not to shame you or make you feel guilty. It is simply to share some insights, raise some questions and make you aware of some possibilities. If you are happy with your life as it is now, fine. Congratulations. I guess you are living the life you always wanted. Or have you simply adjusted your expectations, limited your dreams and decided to settle for what you have?

SUMO wisdom

Do not adjust your goals to bring them in line with your life. Adjust your life to bring it in line with your goals.

If you had more yeses than noes – congratulations. However, whatever your answers, the next few pages will either confirm the kind of future you want or help you to create it.

> *How will you ensure you have no regrets?* Points to
> *How often do you take time out to consider* Ponder...
> *what you really want from life? What will*
> *your legacy be?*

Let's go back to the five questions I asked above. Your answers are the starting point to creating your desired future. And if your future focus seems a little fuzzy at the moment, don't worry. As Zig Ziglar said, 'Go as far as you can and when you get there you'll see further.'

Here, again is the first question.

What does success mean to you?

It is important to come up with your own definition of success rather than focus on what you think other people see it as. People can be caught in the trap of living their life to please others rather than the life they choose. In such cases success is hollow and ultimately unfulfilling.

To help you focus on what success means to you, I would encourage you to read the next piece of 'The personal stuff' and then the lessons that follow.

THE PERSONAL STUFF

I used to have a warped and unbalanced view of success. I had never consciously considered what success meant to me, but on reflection, two areas were important: how much I earned and how much I weighed. Mistakenly I believed that if I achieved a certain level of income and was a particular weight, then I would be successful. And achieving success, I assumed, would equate to being happy. I was wrong. Very wrong. On 24 December 1997 my wife and I embarked upon our usual Christmas Eve ritual. After our children went to bed (they were aged four and two at the time) we would share a meal together and exchange a couple of presents. It was an opportunity to reflect back on the year, to talk about our highs and lows and share our hopes for the coming year. But this time was different. I was in a relatively upbeat mood. This had been a good year. I had achieved my financial goals, completed another book and was within a couple of pounds of my ideal weight. Not only that, but I had spoken in Hong Kong, Malaysia and Singapore and visited (on my own) a family friend in Australia.

Helen's view of the year was very different. It had been a year when she and the children had seen very little of me. When I was at home my whole focus was work-related and I had become increasingly irritable with her and the children. All that seemed to matter to me was what was going on in my world. Was I successful in business? Yes. Was I being a good husband and father? No. If things continued unchanged for the next couple of years would we remain married? Unlikely. I had been blind to my behaviour and the impact my attitude was having on my family. Finally, Helen explained what things looked like from her side of the beachball. It was the wake-up call I needed. It was time to broaden my definition of success.

Broadening your definition of success

As a result of this experience I identified four key aspects of my life that I needed to keep a check on. Although I list them separately, they are not independent of each other. They all interrelate in some way and are all equally important. The first one is optional depending on your circumstances. If this is the case, you may want to view it as 'work', which may be paid or unpaid.

1   *Career*. I also include finance in this area. My business is still very important to me and I do still spend time away from home. But my view of work has changed. It is no longer the sole definition of who I am as a person. I have learnt to take myself a little less seriously, to delegate more and to learn the art of saying 'no' when appropriate. Previously, my family's needs came further

down my list of priorities than my clients. I would never admit to this of course, but my behaviour revealed the truth. I didn't even realize it. My clients and cash flow are still important, but so too are my family. My desire for work–life fulfilment (which I believe is a more helpful term than work–life balance) came about through a change in my attitude. I need to focus on my career but not to the detriment of the rest of my life.

2   *Relationships.* I had taken my family for granted and when I was at home, my mind was still on work. I now appreciate how fortunate I am. Now I do not just plan my work, I plan family activities. When the children were younger this did not simply include holidays or a weekend away, but what I term 'family nights'. No phone calls were answered, no friends came round after school. This was simply our time together. We enjoyed a favourite meal and either a DVD or a few games.

My children's age and mobile phones mean such an idyllic evening is no longer the norm, but we still plan meals together for just the four of us. What would that look like for you with your family?

My relationship with friends is also important. They help me see things in perspective and are very good at helping me keep my feet firmly on the ground. Fun time with friends is now crucial for me.

Remember, the quality of your relationships underpins all you do. (A group called the Relationships Foundation has coined the term 'Relationship Pension'. The idea is that if we are to have a fulfilled life in the future, we not only need to invest our finances, but also invest in our relationships. They can be contacted at http://www .relationshipsfoundation.org/.)

3   *Recreation*. I include health and leisure time in this dimension of my life. Health, for me, incorporates my physical, psychological and spiritual well-being. My faith is fundamental to who I am as a person, and I value time to reflect, to pray and to enjoy moments of silence. When I exercise either by going for long walks or visits to the gym, it helps my physical and mental well-being. My times of recreation literally provide opportunities to 're-create'. This next point is more important now than it's ever been.

To thrive in a demanding, fast-paced world, we all need times of recovery and moments to relax.They should not be seen as optional extras, but as priorities. Here's a reminder of a point I made in the preface to this book: When you travel on a plane, during the safety announcements, they make the following point: 'If there's a drop in cabin pressure, the oxygen masks will come down.' But now take note of what is then said: 'Put your own mask on first before helping others.' Recreation and recovery time for us is crucial if we're to be fulfilled and successful in both our personal and professional lives. It's our opportunity to put our own mask on first so that we're then in a better place to help others. Let's get real here. How successful can you be if you're burnt out and exhausted?

4   *Contribution*. My life had become so self-absorbed I rarely considered the needs of others. But I have since discovered the strangest secret: it really can be better to give than to receive.

That is what contribution is about. I feel more fulfilled now that I view my time, talent and money not just as an opportunity to meet my needs, but also those of others. It is quite liberating when you become less inward-looking. Making a contribution to others, in whatever way, makes you feel better about yourself.

Reviewing these four equally important dimensions of who I am and what I do is a good 'life check'. It is a process I go through regularly, usually on a monthly basis. For you to enjoy a fulfilled life I would recommend you do the same. Here's a reminder of the four quadrants:

Career/Work   Relationships

ME

Recreation   Contribution

SUMO wisdom

Even when your car is running well, it's still good to have it serviced. The same goes for your life. When did you last have a check-up?

So what about you? Consider what success means to you, in relation to the following:

- *Career* (or your paid or unpaid work) – Success means…
- *Relationships* – Success means…
- *Recreation* – Success means…
- *Contribution* – Success means…

OK, now, let's go on to look at the second question…

Do you have some clearly defined goals that you wish to achieve in life?

It is good to have goals. They provide focus, direction, motivation, purpose and feedback. They can be in any area of our lives. Trust me, when times are tough – the traffic is bad, the builders are late and the boss is being difficult – your ability to cope will improve if there is something you are aiming for that is bigger than all those challenges.

Review the Career, Relationships, Recreation and Contribution aspects of your life. Set yourself a goal in each area. Let's start with the short term. What would you like to achieve in the next three months? Write down your goals below.

1　My Career (or work) goal over the next three months is…
2　My Relationship goal over the next three months is…
3　My Recreation goal over the next three months is…
4　My Contribution goal over the next three months is…

Now let's think long term. Dream a little if you like and come up with the top ten things you want to do before you leave this planet.

Top ten things to do before I leave this planet

1
2
3
4
5
6
7
8
9
10

Vicky, a delegate on one of my workshops, did a similar exercise. She decided on the ten things she wanted to do during the next year. Included in her top ten were: spending a night at the Ritz Hotel in London; riding a horse; having her hair styled at Vidal Sassoon; and raising money for charity by running the London Marathon. There is nothing especially out of the ordinary about these goals and there doesn't have to be. Your goals simply need to be meaningful for you and motivate you to take action.

SUMO wisdom

Unfortunate are those without goals. For they drift along helping someone else to achieve theirs.

THE PERSONAL STUFF

In 1996 I wrote down in some detail the house I wanted to live in. I knew the location I wanted, the type of garden, the number of bedrooms and the need for a kitchen big enough to eat in as a family. And I wanted a conservatory. The house we bought four years later did not have all we wanted but it was in the right location and had the right size garden. Two years later, with the help of an extension, we achieved our desired outcome. And, as you know, it included a conservatory! The future can be yours to see, but you need to plan for it.

Having decided what you want to do, the following questions will help you clarify how to make your goals a reality.

The third question is…

Have you shared your goals with someone close to you?

It is important you do not set goals in isolation. How supportive are those closest to you about your goals? When I was thinking of my ideal house, Helen, my wife, had some different ideas from me. Fortunately, we agreed on most things, which was just as well, as we wanted to carry on living together. It has also been important that Helen supports my business goals, which, to be achieved, will mean my being away from home on a regular basis.

Likewise, I need to be aware she has some goals that require my support. We may need to give and take a little on occasions and make some compromises. But it is far better for a long-term, healthy relationship if we consider the needs of each other rather than single-mindedly pursuing our own objectives.

The fourth question is…

Do you have some plans in place to help you achieve your goals?

I regularly hear people say 'Well, we hope one day to…' or, 'Maybe one day we will have enough money to…'. Can I be blunt about this?

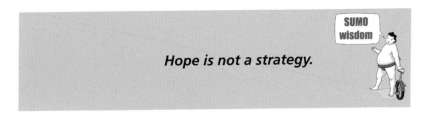

Hope is not a strategy.

SUMO wisdom

Forget the phrase 'Show me the money' – I say, 'First show me the plan'. What's your strategy going to be to achieve your goals? Here are some questions to help you focus on what you want to achieve and how to go about making it a reality.

1   Why is this goal important to you? If you do not have a strong enough reason, your commitment to achieving your goal will be lessened. There is no point setting a half-hearted goal just for the sake of it.
2   What will it mean to you personally to achieve this goal? How will you feel when you reach your desired outcome?
3   Make an honest assessment of where you are currently in relation to your goal. Is it realistic to achieve your outcome and, if so, in what time scale? (Setting yourself a target to earn a million pounds in the next six months when you are currently in debt and there is no business opportunity on the horizon is not impossible, but it's worth a reality check. And wanting to run a marathon in the next three months when you are currently struggling to climb the stairs is not advisable.) This is not a call to lower your aspirations, but be aware of the following:

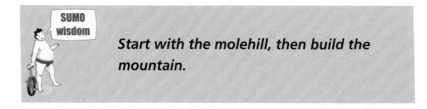

SUMO wisdom

Start with the molehill, then build the mountain.

I think it is fantastic to dream big, but it is useful to start small. The first talk I ever gave was to a church youth group. Due to the evening running later than planned, my 'Thought For The Day' slot was reduced from five minutes to thirty seconds. Although I dreamed of speaking internationally, I started my speaking career in a church hall a mile away from home.

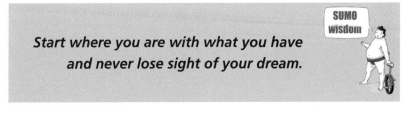

SUMO wisdom

Start where you are with what you have and never lose sight of your dream.

Anthony Robbins offers a useful insight:

'People tend to overestimate what they can achieve in a year, but underestimate what they can achieve in a lifetime.'

4   What resources do you need to help you achieve your goal? Resources could be in the form of equipment, money, time, information and people. People are perhaps your biggest resource. They can provide you with advice, introduce you to the appropriate contacts and support you in your journey. List your resources here:

The resources I need to help me achieve my goal:

5   Plan your plan. What needs to happen now? What is your next step and what about the one after that? What are your time scales?

The above is all well and good if you do it. It's more likely to happen if you have a 'mate' to work through your answers with, and to whom you can be accountable.

SUMO wisdom

Seeking support isn't a sign of weakness. It's a sign of wisdom.

THE PERSONAL STUFF

My goal was to write a book that incorporated the SUMO success principles that I had been speaking about through my work. This is the book you are now reading. In order to achieve this outcome I sought the help of my friend Steve. He suggested which publishers to approach and how best to pitch my proposal. I shared this goal with the people close to me, including my family, friends and colleagues from my industry. Having done so, I felt even more focused on making it a reality. I researched the publishers, started gathering my ideas and then began writing.

Along the journey I have had to deal with rejection as well as interest from publishers. I have listened to people challenge my ideas as well as support them. I have needed to write when I felt little or no inspiration and to see my task not as writing a book, but writing a page, followed by another page and then another. Not only have I been writing about the SUMO success principles, but I have been seeking to apply them as well. Rejection has brought the temptation to try on the Victim T-shirt. I have resisted. Just. But I have appreciated the need to have a little Hippo Time with myself. I have heard the Inner Critic on numerous occasions but I have decided not to entertain him as a guest.

This has only been possible due to the support and encouragement of others. In fact without it, this book would never have been completed. I have Remembered the Beachball and sought the views of several people for their perspective on each chapter. They have seen 'sides' to each principle that I had not considered; they have given me insights into my own material that I had failed to notice.

I have also needed to remind myself on several occasions why writing this book is so important to me. There are several reasons, including a desire to see the SUMO message spread beyond the people who hear me speak. I confess I also want the book to raise my profile, which, in my business, is especially important. I also want to leave a legacy to my children, my grandchildren and their grandchildren. Though they may never meet me face to face, I hope they encounter me through the written pages. I love the following quote, 'If you want to live an immortal life, do something worth remembering'. I've found that hugely inspiring whilst writing this book. Deep down I think we all want to be remembered for something.

Points to Ponder...

This is a little of my story on the journey to achieving my goal. It's an insight into some of the events along the way and how I've responded. Because of those responses you're now reading the outcome (E + R = O). What will your story be? How will you use the SUMO principles to help you achieve success? What do you need to be aware of that could be an obstacle to your progress?

Finally, the fifth question…

What kind of memories would you like your family and friends to have of you?

Write below what you believe they would say. If you are struggling, you might want to ask them. If you think there are not as many happy memories as you would like, then it is up to you to change that.

At the moment my family's memories of me would include:

In the future, I'd also like them to remember me because of:

At the moment my friends' memories of me would include:

In the future, I'd also like them to remember me because of:

In a nutshell

Designing your life and creating circumstances rather than reacting to them is not always easy. To do so means not simply reading about these SUMO principles, but living them as well.

It begins when we 'Change our T-shirt' and acknowledge that if life is not as we want it, then creating a different future is down to us. It means taking charge of our thinking. Our thinking ultimately creates our results. When you want to make changes in life, 'faulty thinking' will anchor you to your old way of behaving. 'Fruity Thinking' will release you to move forward. Use the seven questions in Chapter 3 to help your journey.

When setbacks occur, as they inevitably will, remember that 'Hippo Time is OK'. Don't deny your frustration or disappointment. Remember, successful people do not go around succeeding all the time. Hippo Time can be helpful, but it can also hinder you. It is part of the journey – it is not a destination. Be careful who you spend it with and remember to *Move On*.

Appreciate that your journey is a much richer experience when you engage the support of others. Remind yourself that understanding their view of the beachball will enhance the quality of your relationships. Never forget that life is not simply about getting your needs met, but helping other people meet theirs. Never underestimate the incredible importance of listening and seeking to understand others.

Use the 'Learn Latin' principle to develop the motivation and momentum to move on. Remember, one of the biggest obstacles to overcoming any challenge is the first step. So just start. And make sure you have a mate to help you along the way. And remember – don't count your days. Make your days count.

Finally, 'Ditch Doris Day'. What your future looks like is largely down to you. Widen your definition of success and recognize that a more fulfilling future awaits you when you focus on your Career, Relationships, Recreation and Contribution.

And above all, in all things, remember to SUMO!

- Shut *Up* the 'whatever will be, will be' attitude and *Move On* to creating your own future.
- Don't wait until it's too late to decide how to live the rest of your days.
- If you want more success in life, define what that means to you.
- Shut *Up* a narrow view of success and *Move On* to broaden your definition.
- Make sure you give your own life a regular service.
- Work–life fulfilment comes when we pay attention to our Career (or work), Relationships, Recreation and Contribution.
- Don't live your life by default. Set goals to create a sense of purpose and direction in your life.
- Create memories worth remembering.
- Dream big, start small.
- Shut *Up* believing success will just happen, *Move On* to developing a plan to create it.
- Use all six SUMO principles to create the future you want to see.

SUMO SUMMARY

The Personal Postscript

Ten years on from first writing this book so much seems to have changed. Not just in the world, but in my own personal life. The SUMO philosophy has opened up so many new opportunities for me. One included sharing a stage with the late Dr Stephen Covey, author of the book *7 Habits of Highly Effective People*. As a result of that talk at the Sydney Convention Centre I have gone on to work in one of my favourite countries on the planet, Australia.

But perhaps one of the most memorable days of my life, which came about as a result of the book, was when I got a chance to spend a day in Kibera, just outside Nairobi in Kenya. Kibera is reputed to be the largest slum area in the whole of the African continent. Along with my friend Paul Sandham I had the privilege to deliver the SUMO message in two schools and a college within Kibera. We even distributed SUMO books to teachers.

The day was memorable, though, for the conversation I had with Felix, the headteacher in one of the schools. He was desperate for me to talk to his pupils. I, however, felt a little uncomfortable doing so. The reason was simply this: many of the children had no shoes. Their uniforms were more like poorly sewn together rags. I remarked, 'Felix, what these children need is shoes and new uniforms, not me talking to them'.

'Wrong,' replied Felix. 'We can get new shoes and uniforms, but what you bring is hope and inspiration. These children need to change their beliefs about who they are and where they're heading.'

And I'll never forget his next words: 'They need to realize they may have been born in a slum, but they don't need to die in a slum.'

I'm guessing most of you are not faced with the same challenges as Felix and his pupils. But we still all face situations that can be incredibly challenging: ill health, redundancy, the loss of a loved one, the breakdown of a long-term relationship. None of us are immune from any of these. But what I hope the SUMO approach does is to equip and encourage you to deal with such situations with greater self-compassion, confidence and increased courage.

Along the way we will make mistakes but, as I learnt from Felix, wherever we're at now doesn't have to be our final destination. The journey continues, and we can create a better future whatever our current circumstances.

For some of you, though, life is rather good as it is. Great. Just remember, SUMO is not just to help you deal with challenges, but to help you and others get the very best from this journey called life.

One of the definitions for the word 'inspire' is 'to breathe life into'. I sincerely hope that you join the many people before you who have read this book and felt inspired. And, just as you put your own oxygen mask on first, I hope the SUMO message inspires you now to help others.

Let me leave you with this thought. You may remember watching quiz shows when the contestant fails to win the main prize. At the end of the programme, the still-smiling quiz master proclaims 'Look what you could have won', as the major prize (often a boat or a motor car) is revealed. The contestant forces a smile, but the disappointment can be seen in their eyes. At the end of my show on this planet, I don't want to be told, 'Look what you could have won. Look what you could have done. Look what you could have become.'

I sincerely hope SUMO helps you to create and enjoy an even better life than you have now. I hope it helps you achieve better relationships with others and inspires you to attempt things you only ever dreamed of doing. I hope, above all, it leaves you looking back on your life and saying, 'Look what I've won, look what I've done, look who I've become'.

It's not an easy journey, as I have already found, but it's a journey worth taking. Enjoy it.

Let me know how SUMO helps:

email Paul.McGee@theSUMOguy.com

or tweet @thesumoguy.

Carpe diem.

Paul McGee

Bonus SUMO Wisdom

Since writing the first edition of this book I've continued to enjoy encapsulating thoughts and ideas into bite-sized phrases. A few weeks ago I contacted subscribers to my newsletter, asking them to vote for their favourites from a list of thirteen. Nearly fourteen hundred people replied to my request, and below are the top seven, as voted for by fans of SUMO. I hope you find them thought-provoking and helpful.

The SUMO Seven

1 Seeking support from others is not a sign of weakness. It's a sign of wisdom.
2 If you woke up feeling tired and miserable, remember this: You woke up. Now dust yourself down and seize the day.
3 When you stop learning you stop living. Engage or exist. It's your call.
4 Your silence, denial or avoidance gives approval to the situation.
5 Remember, in order for people to insult you, you first have to value their opinion.
6 Be careful of the tendency to over-glamorize what you don't have and undervalue what you do have.
7 Remember, you're here to make a difference. Not win a popularity contest.

Want To Know More About SUMO?

Please feel free to visit our website **www.theSUMOguy.com** where you can download free articles and tip sheets and learn about other resources available.

You can also subscribe to our newsletter which provides regular 'food for thought' from Paul on a range of issues as well as keeping you up to date on when and where you can hear him speak.

SUMO4Schools

SUMO4Schools provides a range of resources and training that facilitate well-being, promote positive behaviour and develop creativity, thinking and learning skills in schools. Developing Paul's six SUMO principles it seeks to promote emotional intelligence and raise aspirations in children and teachers alike.

This innovative and important programme can be delivered within a cross-curricular context, but most importantly it is fun! Programmes cover both primary and secondary phases.

When working in schools we emphasize the Latin translation of the word SUMO which is 'choose', as well as defining the SUMO acronym as: Stop, Understand, Move On.

For more information visit **www.SUMO4schools.com**

Bring Paul to your organization

Paul McGee speaks at team events and conferences and conducts seminars and masterclasses. He tailors his message to your requirements and is commonly asked to speak on leadership, change, relationships at work, motivation and dealing with stress positively.

You can book Paul or one of his team to deliver the principles of this book inside your organization. For more details about the SUMO programme or any more of Paul's services, either:

n-mail: Paul.McGee@theSUMOguy.com

or visit: www.theSUMOguy.com

If you prefer, you can telephone the offices of PMA International Ltd (Paul's company) on:

tel: +44 (0) 1925 268708

We look forward to hearing from you.

SUMO and Act4Africa

Some people who want to move on in life are hindered through no fault of their own. Therefore I have decided that part of the profits from this book will go to the charity Act4Africa whom I have been involved in working with and supporting since 2003.

About Act4Africa

Established in 2000, Act4Africa is a UK-based charity and a registered NGO.

The charities primary aims are:

- To deliver effective HIV/AIDS prevention education.
- To challenge cultural norms and change attitudes and behaviours.
- To empower women to take control of their sexual health.
- To reduce stigmatization of those living with HIV/AIDS.

Paul working in Kisumu, Kenya.

Enthusiastic support for the work of Act4Africa in Uganda.

Over a ten-year period the charity has gained a demonstrable track record of successfully delivering HIV/AIDS prevention education and HIV counselling and testing programmes in urban and rural communities through its own indigenous Act4Africa teams.

Act4africa Programmes

Act4Africa currently works in Uganda, Tanzania and Malawi, delivering the following programmes:

- Youth Work
- HIV Counselling and Testing (HCT)
- 'Train the Trainer' (ToT)

Working, wherever possible, In partnership with local organizations to deliver the programmes in schools and communities and nationwide, the focus also extends towards reaching high-risk groups, including women, sex workers, prisoners, police camps, the military and fishing communities.

Further Contact

For further information on the work of Act4Africa please visit our website at: www.act4africa.org.

Seven Questions To Help You SUMO

Faced with a challenge?
7 questions to help you
S.U.M.O.

1: Where is this issue on a scale of 1 - 10?

2: How important will this be in 6 months time?

3: Is my response appropriate and effective?

4: How can I influence or improve the situation?

5: What can I learn from this?

6: What will I do differently next time?

7: What can I find that's positive in this situation?

www.paulmcgee.com   Tel: 44 (0) 1925 268 708   E-mail: sumo@paulmcgee.com

Index